Why
Social Movements
Matter

Why
Social Movements
Matter

An Introduction

Laurence Cox

ROWMAN &
LITTLEFIELD
INTERNATIONAL

London • New York

Published by Rowman & Littlefield International Ltd.
Unit A, Whitacre Mews, 26–34 Stannary Street, London SE11 4AB
www.rowmaninternational.com

Rowman & Littlefield International Ltd. is an affiliate of Rowman & Littlefield
4501 Forbes Boulevard, Suite 200, Lanham, Maryland 20706, USA
With additional offices in Boulder, New York, Toronto (Canada), and Plymouth (UK)
www.rowman.com

British Library Cataloguing in Publication Data
A catalogue record for this book is available from the British Library

ISBN: HB 978-1-7866-0781-2
         PB 978-1-7866-0782-9

Library of Congress Cataloging-in-Publication Data

Names: Cox, Laurence, author.
Title: Why social movements matter : an introduction / by Laurence Cox.
Description: Lanham : Rowman & Littlefield International, [2018] | Includes
    bibliographical references and index.
Identifiers: LCCN 2018005953 (print) | LCCN 2018010949 (ebook) | ISBN
    9781786607836 (electronic) | ISBN 9781786607812 (cloth : alk. paper) |
    ISBN 9781786607829 (pbk. : alk. paper)
Subjects: LCSH: Social movements—History. | Social movements—Political
    aspects.
Classification: LCC HM881 (ebook) | LCC HM881 .C69 2018 (print) |
    DDC 303.48/4—dc23
LC record available at https://lccn.loc.gov/2018005953

♾™ The paper used in this publication meets the minimum requirements of American
National Standard for Information Sciences – Permanence of Paper for Printed Library
Materials, ANSI/NISO Z39.48–1992.

Printed in the United States of America

Contents

Introduction

Since the turn of the twenty-first century, social movements have been a constantly active presence in many different countries and continents. In the US, the dramatic struggles of Black Lives Matter against the de facto freedom of police forces to kill young black men, expressing the limited effect of the Obama election, fed into a much wider set of struggles against the Trump administration, showing just how varied social movements can be: from the Women's Marches of 21 January 2017 to individuals and groups from all sorts of previously mainstream backgrounds resigning or resisting the new regime's policies; from flash mobs at airports welcoming Muslims via coordinated resistance to immigration raids; and from new forms of anti-fascist action on the streets and online to the anti-pipeline struggles at Standing Rock and elsewhere.

In Canada and more recently the US, indigenous opposition to petroleum pipelines and tar sands extraction has increasingly been successful in facing down an industry traditionally seen as nearly unstoppable. Further south, the indigenous-based Zapatista revolution has successfully held onto its liberated zones in the Lacandon jungle for over twenty-four years, encouraging and supporting movements against neoliberalism – the most recent, and most aggressive, form of capitalism – around the world. In South America, powerful indigenous movements fed into the shaping of new kinds of state in Bolivia and Ecuador in particular, but which they have increasingly found themselves in conflict with. Elsewhere, a 'pink tide' saw powerful movement struggles, from the Argentinian revolution of 2001 to the Brazilian labour and landless movements, help put left governments of many different kinds in power, a process now being rolled back against huge popular resistance: perhaps 35 million people in Brazil's 2017 general strike.

In China, there are massive levels of labour unrest in its new factory zones, together with constant rural conflicts over land and environmental issues, while Tibetan self-immolation and Hong Kong pro-democracy activism continue. In India, the struggles of tribal Adivasis and of *dalits* outside the caste system cross with women's struggles against rape and dowry killings, while the peasant uprising in the 'Red Corridor' forms the target for a vicious counter-insurgency campaign. In South Africa, popular struggles against the corruption and continuing inequalities of African National Congress (ANC) rule have led to increasing independence in the labour movement, which became visible in the 2012 state massacre of mineworkers at Marikana, while the shanty towns are the site of new kinds of struggle against privatisation and against clientelistic power.

In the Middle East and North Africa, long-standing tensions around Palestine and resistance to the war in Iraq fed, alongside labour struggles, democratic and feminist activism and forms of popular Islamism, into the wave of uprisings of 2011, with a series of outcomes ranging from violent repression in Bahrain via the return of military rule in Egypt to Tunisia's more hopeful process of change. Meanwhile, the uprising of Gezi Park and the growth of a new left in Turkey have been met with a vicious crackdown. In the chaos of the Syrian civil war, the radical-democratic and feminist struggle of Rojava's Kurds has won the world's attention. Across Europe, refugees fleeing the war provoked a wave of popular solidarity and direct action while racist movements have used the situation to boost their own power.

On the European periphery, Iceland's 'saucepan revolution' of 2008–2009 and the dramatic Greek challenge to EU austerity from 2007 to 2015 form part of a wide variety of popular experiments alongside the huge anti-authoritarian movements in Spain and the Catalan conflict, more conventional forms of protest in Portugal and Ireland's widespread and sustained community-based resistance to the introduction of water meters. Elsewhere, the extraordinary democratic experience of Nuit Debout in France and the movement takeover of the British Labour Party through Momentum contrast with the rise of far-right and racist movements across much of Europe – along with a thousand other struggles, large and small, ranging from workplace conflict to direct action against destructive development, from climate change organising to solidarity with refugees.

Social movements, then, are everywhere – both geographically and in the different parts of the social order. They are defeated or decline as well as having their moments of winning. They are not all nice, or right. They are creative and unpredictable, resisting the lazy generalisations of journalists under deadline pressure.

In many ways, it is this last point which is hardest to take on board: movements are widespread and frequent but *not routine*, running throughout the social world and across societies but *not homogenous*. It is, after all,

Coca-Cola or Vodafone which tries to sell the exact same thing with a series of branches run on identical managerial principles in different cities and languages. When movements organise, even if they ally across countries, the people involved do not do the same thing in the same way everywhere. They do not transmit a top-down policy decision, but have to work out in many different times and places, under all sorts of pressures and with very different aims and ideas, how they should proceed. This diversity, changeability and internal contradiction is part of what makes them fascinating to study seriously, and hard to describe without making a real effort.

WHY MOVEMENTS AREN'T EASY TO WRITE ABOUT

One indication of how hard it is to talk about movements in mainstream intellectual genres is to note the jump in form that comes when movements appear. Thus, protests might appear on the dust jacket or the illustrations of a book about political economy whose analysis is relentlessly structural in focus, or as the opening anecdote to an article whose real purpose is to present as natural or unchangeable the very inequalities protested against in the anecdote. A systematic analysis of institutional injustice may end with a brief moment of moral outrage and a gesture towards the need for radical change with no serious discussion of how to achieve this. Or the phrase 'social movements' may appear as a sort of black box, mysteriously bridging the gap between the world as it is and the world as it should be.

What all of these express is that conventional intellectual forms routinely *break down* when faced with movements; or conversely that the only role movements can play within them is to perform tasks which their own main focus cannot – get the audience interested, bring a dry subject to life, paper over the cracks in a deterministic analysis or deal with the awkward fact that yet another sociological exposé of the horrors of the world will not actually motivate policy makers to change anything.

At other times, otherwise careful scholars reach for the most clichéd accounts of movements, whether political or academic in origin, or dismiss them with the laziest of analyses. Four pages of the German social theorist Jürgen Habermas on the subject, for example, have been quite enough to supply many a 'critical' analysis, despite his own practical inability to engage sensibly with movements in his own 'lifeworld': in 1968, he described the new university movements as constituting a 'left fascism', perhaps for asking too many critical questions about professorial power. Serious journalists who would not dream of writing about judicial reform or electoral strategy without doing their homework are only too happy to fill column inches with the most basic misunderstandings about what movements want, think and do.

There are, though, good reasons why what the Italian communist leader Antonio Gramsci called 'traditional intellectuals' – those trained for and working in conventional forms of knowledge production – find it hard to think seriously about social movements. First, at a personal level, their own acquaintance with movements is often just a brief period in college, maybe encountering people who were trying hard to *act* like activists – and perhaps, in retrospect, embarrassed by their own unsuccessful attempts to adopt the same roles, or needing to justify their own life choices.

There have been times and places when it was possible to move between being an effective activist to being a successful film director, novelist, academic or journalist – but in the normal course of events, a successful career in these highly prestigious and (at the top) well-rewarded professions requires a fair degree of instrumental ruthlessness as well as the ability to impress those who control the distribution of money, power and cultural capital in these milieux. Small wonder then that novelists' accounts of movement activism are more likely to be caricatures than credible. The profuse thanks often given at the end of police procedurals to professionals on that side of the barricades are rarely found in novels featuring social movements, mostly not to protect the innocent but rather because authors do not feel the need to be remotely as well-informed about activists. The exceptions are rare enough to underline the rule.

Second, in practice, traditional intellectuals' relationship to 'society as a whole' tends towards a stronger identification with society *as it is*, whether lightly modified in a positive direction or in decline from a conservative golden age. This is, after all, what they are trained in: to assemble the money for a Hollywood movie, it is important to convince nervous investors that a movie will appeal to large North American and west European audiences and to the Asian middle classes. To become a professor, it is important to seem suitably professorial to the managerial class who run present-day universities. To win prizes as a novelist, it is important to respect the boundaries of the novel as a high-status genre. To become a successful journalist, it is important to understand the ins and outs of institutional business as usual, whether that be parliamentary politics or the financial markets.

It is not, of course, that nobody is capable of getting through these barriers and still saying something more radical; it is that the routine mode of discourse in all of these fields is one in which social movements are not significant. Even more strongly, when movements do appear, professional success consists in boiling them down for Important Intellectual Matters, in other words reasserting one's own cultural capital: inserting a brief political interlude within a novel of character and perception, within a discussion of the prospects of a new leadership for a mainstream party, within an art-house movie or within a Serious Work on economics.

Third, and perhaps most important, the normal form of traditional intellectual discourse is usually bird's-eye description – 'this is how the world is' – or moral exhortation – 'this is how it should be'. If there is a space for what we should do, that 'we' is not a radical collective acting without access to power, wealth and cultural authority: it is a national 'we', a 'we' composed of right-thinking people or those who share the same elevated cultural tastes, a 'we' of those who actually decide what happens in society or a 'we' of an imagined cultural unity. It is, in some ways, by *successfully* making such appeals to 'we' (success meaning not that action is taken, but that the appeal is recognised as a worthy one) that one ratifies one's position as a traditional intellectual.

There are, of course, cruder reasons for not talking about movements, or only doing so in caricatured ways. Chomsky and Herman's 'five filters' outline how this works in journalism: concentrated media ownership; dependence on advertisers; reliance on material provided by the state, business and associated experts; 'flak' making life difficult for critical journalists and anti-communism. More generally, traditional intellectuals almost always work within hierarchical institutions in which their job, their promotion or their next engagement depends on pleasing people above them, who are in turn closer to power, cultural authority and sheer wealth. Given what social movements are, it is hardly surprising that (at the most basic) the only way to advance one's career while mentioning movements is to misrepresent them.

The level of discussion of movements in these contexts is often so poor that we have to start by clarifying something about what social movements are, and are not. Of course there are genuine issues of definition, some of which will appear in this book. But that does not mean that there are not simple *mis*-understandings, and it is important to get some of these out of the way first.

WHAT MOVEMENTS ARE, AND WHAT THEY AREN'T

At a naïve level, movements are often understood as 'something ordinary people do in numbers', whether that means consuming some kind of food, voting in a particular way, wearing particular clothes, reading particular books or whatever. Any of these *can* form part of movements, if there is some form of collective organisation behind them: vegetarianism, for example, or a candidate backed by movement organisations; styles or ideas too can be produced within movements and then commodified, brought into a different set of social relations (a familiar process in music, bringing its own tensions between movement and mainstream relationships).

Less wide of the mark, an organisation (perhaps an NGO or a party), an individual (perhaps a political figure or a writer) or a group working on a particular issue is sometimes identified with or described as a movement, at times by those involved. There have been times and places where a single organisation, often with a centralised leadership, formed the backbone of a whole movement: in the mid-twentieth century, this was often true for anti-colonial nationalisms as for social democracy or communism, and fascism was also capable of using the term 'movement' in this way. Today, it is still possible to find organisations with the term 'movement' in their name, varying from political parties to anarchist groups and from trade unions to mildly political forms of development work.

To understand social movements, though, we need to put the emphasis above all on the people involved in creating this collective agency, in whatever way, and to ask about the relationships between them. In other words, we look for the networks – formal and clientelistic or informal and radically democratic, with many other shades in between – that *connect* different kinds of formal organisation and informal group, parties and trade unions, cultural figures and politicians and even (in some cases) churches, online media, subcultures, everyday forms of resistance, popular memories of past revolutions or lifestyles. There is no particular, privileged form through which people come together in movements: or rather, in different times and places, in different movements and traditions, people do these things differently.

What makes something a movement rather than something else is above all *conflict*: movements develop (and argue over) a sense of 'we' which is opposed to a 'they' (the state, corporations, a powerful social group, a form of behaviour) in a conflict which is about the shape and direction of society, on a large or small scale in terms of geography but also in terms of the scope of the issue. In social movement, then, society, or some part of it, *moves*, or tries to. As we shall see, part of this moving is also a process either of building alliances and hence 'scaling-up' the way an issue is thought about (from defending children against respiratory diseases caused by car exhausts to tackling a whole way of structuring industrial society), or of breaking down into more particularist spaces (villages resisting incinerators set against villages resisting new landfill dumps, for example).

Precisely because movements seek to *move*, they can also change their field of operations: retreating into forms of everyday grumbling, quiet resistance and popular memory in times of defeat, advancing into political challenges or mass direct action in times when success seems possible; even, in periods that shake the world, overturning the existing state and remaking it, or making another kind of society, not always within the same borders. If there is one thing movements are not, it is dull and predictable: if they settle into routines for a few years, they rarely have the resources that in other kinds of social activity keep people behaving in the same way over decades with only minimal changes. Movements, as we shall see in this book, involve people thinking *hard* and *creatively* about how to win against opponents who are often more powerful, wealthier and with greater cultural authority than them. This is one of the things that makes them such a delight to participate in and to study – they are among the spaces where people push themselves most fully, in more dimensions of their being than in more narrowly defined contexts.

LEARNING FROM EACH OTHER'S STRUGGLES

I have been lucky enough to spend my life around movements in many different ways. I grew up in a world of social movements, lively enough to hear the occasional click on the phone line or wonder about the men sitting in a car outside the house, and have vivid memories of knocking on doors, stuffing envelopes and rattling tins – activities which form the baseline of much movement activity. Later on, I became active in more independent ways and explored many different kinds of activism, from NGOs to direct action, from student politics to community organising and from small projects to networking across struggles. I was able to spend time around movements in different countries and to meet political exiles from many more. All of this helped me to think about social movements not as a thing but as a human activity, about the different ways in which we inhabit and give life to movements, what we do with them and who we become in the process.

As a student, I was introduced to the wider world of the history of the French revolutions and the place of left, far left and green parties in 1980s Europe. I researched Hamburg's social movement milieu and the Irish counterculture as a participant and through all of this encountered many more ways of thinking about movements, both activist and academic, though at the time these approaches often had little contact with one another. For over two decades I have been lucky enough to work mainly on social movements in my research and teaching.

I have remained involved in movements throughout but in a very wide range of different situations, each challenging in its own different way. Through the Manchester Alternative Futures and Popular Protest conference and the open-access journal *Interface*, I have had the privilege of working with some of the most interesting activist researchers in social movements on the planet and contributing to the project of developing better conversations between the sharpest forms of movement theorising and the most engaged forms of academic research in the area. I have also taught many activists in the university, and learned a lot from the experience. This 'ecology of knowledges' has continually forced me to think harder, and not remain satisfied with simple answers to the complexity of movement realities.

For some time now I have wanted to step back from my more specific work in the area to say something about movements for a wider audience, in response to their near-total *absence* in so many of the social institutions which claim to represent human beings to themselves but instead wind up presenting us with an official vision of the world in which popular struggle is neatly airbrushed out of the picture. (It is telling that acknowledging the presence of massive unemployment, institutional abuse or torture is far less socially threatening than is acknowledging the presence of large numbers of determined people seeking to change the social relations that give rise to these things.)

And yet somehow, despite blackout or caricature from the dominant institutions of intellectual production, movements do manage to articulate themselves and their activity below the radar, and people do come to hear about them, if often only in fragmentary ways. This book is intended as a contribution to that discussion, not around any specific social movement but rather around movement activism as such, and the broader possibility of a better life. Politically, this book seeks to help the process of learning from each other's struggles, which is one of the most important things I think we can do in trying to strengthen and radicalise our own activity in movements. Intellectually, it seeks to articulate some elements of what I think can be learned from those struggles about how to change the world for the better.

TALKING WITH THE BARMAN ABOUT ACTIVISM

I work as an academic, but at one point I nearly wound up becoming the barman for the Dublin left. Many years ago, a solidarity centre I had good connections with was thinking about finding a new space of its own, and funding it through running a café. Together with some comrades, I agreed to take on the café project. In true Dublin style, things did not go quite as planned: at an early point, someone set fire to the pile of furniture that another café had given us in return for our help with renovation, and the project was eventually abandoned. I like to think that I could have been a good barman, and that I could have helped make a collective café a welcoming space for all sorts of different movements in Dublin.

This book tells a few of my own bar stories where they might be helpful, not so much because they are particularly unusual (they aren't), but because they illustrate the often very everyday nature of social movement activism. More interestingly, it draws on the many different conversations (in bars and otherwise) I have had with other activists, whether listening directly to their stories and ideas, or learning indirectly about them from other researchers.

I have written the book as a series of conversations, or for three overlapping audiences. First, there is a conversation with people who are outraged at the state of the world and want to do something about it but – in the late 2010s – find it hard to believe in the real possibility of doing so. Chapter 1 talks about why we need movements, for people who feel very distant from them. Chapter 2 steps back to talk more about history, and particularly how movements have created the world we live in.

Second, there is a conversation with people who understand themselves as being on the left, progressive or radical in various ways, but do not connect that directly with social movements. Chapter 3 talks about this wider political perspective on changing the world and why movements are, or should be, central to it.

Third, there is a conversation with academics and students *outside* social movement studies or who are starting to study it, aiming to encourage them to think more systematically about where movements come in, both in their intellectual questions and their own lives and motivations. Chapter 4 talks about what it means to orient your thinking systematically towards practice, joining up theory and study on the one hand with collective social action on the other. Chapter 5 talks about the relationship between social movements and intellectual activity, particularly in universities. Finally, the conclusion discusses what we might need, in this dark time in world history, to keep going and to take on the forces gathered against us. Each of these chapters has its own style: I hope readers will enjoy the changes of gear.

ABOUT THIS BOOK

I hope the reader will be convinced that it is worth thinking further about some things.

Most importantly, we can and should take our outrage at the world seriously and translate it into action. In the early 1790s, William Blake wrote, '[S]he who desires but acts not breeds pestilence'. If we experience ourselves or those we love, strangers whose suffering we care about or the world we value as being attacked, diminished, oppressed, exploited, threatened or stigmatised, then taking action is an emotionally healthy response – and if we are to have an effect, that action needs to be collective. If we experience these things and do not respond, we are likely to find that we become depressed or bitter and cynical, resentful or out only for ourselves – and in all these cases living a shallower life in which we are not able to fully acknowledge or act on our justified emotions.

But, in order to respond effectively, it helps to recognise how common social movements are and how often they are at least partly successful – far more commonly so than most diet or self-help books, for example. Recognising this reality does not involve thinking that there are any guarantees of success, that everyone we meet in movements is a saint or that there are no costs or risks. It simply involves seeing movements as lying within our normal, everyday sphere of action rather than leaving them 'out there' as an impossible option.

Another key point is that movements are not just widespread in the present day, but have also shaped much of the landscape we live in and move through. So rich is this heritage that it can be hard to see the wood for the trees; and this is particularly true for that part of this heritage which understands itself as The Left, at one time 'the memory of the class' but now, all too often, something rather different. Indeed, as we shall see, 'the left' as a term is a question rather than a definition; it is used to mean everything from 'right-thinking readers of centre-left media' via 'members of a particular intellectual world' to 'a particular set of radical parties and groups'. I will argue that we should think of 'the left' as bringing together the best of movement experience, organising and action. Without attacking comrades and companer@s who are doing incredible work under difficult circumstances, I want to suggest some ways in which organising politics entirely around the expression of *opinions* in the media, and fetishising political parties as an organising form, are both unhelpful to a better relationship between the left and movements.

Last, movements offer and have offered a fundamental resource for serious intellectual work, academic and activist alike, around the shape of our societies and how to change them; but taking this seriously on board involves systematically questioning conventional academic and mainstream habits of thought. I will argue that a different kind of intellectual work is possible in which the relationship between thought-in-dialogue and collective practice is less alienated, more honest and fundamentally *better* – better intellectually, better ethically and better politically.

These are large claims, and this is a small book. But if I am right that collective agency is far more central than we think to everyday life, they do not involve asking people to engage in something 'other' so much as to transform what is an often alienated relationship to present-day experience. Moreover, we are right to test propositions against our 'experience' – a term made famous by the great English historian of social movements, E. P. Thompson – in using what we read and hear to think more deeply about the needs we are already conscious of, our existing attempts to meet them and how we understand what we are up to and where we are going. Thus I am not, in this short essay, trying to drag the reader onto an intellectual field set up in such a way that I can 'prove' these claims; rather, I want to engage in a conversation in which I hope the reader will hear something that she (or he) can respond to and which will perhaps help them in their own struggles.

THANKS AND APOLOGIES

This book distils a lifetime of conversations, joint organising projects, radical educational initiatives, scholarly arguments – and more than a little of the intellectual version of shouting at the telly. I am immensely indebted to a very wide range of fellow activists, community organisers, students, colleagues and friends for the ideas we have developed in conversation. Elsewhere I have tried to name individually everyone whose ideas I am aware of as having fed into a particular specific discussion, but to do so here would mean doubling the length of a book which argues that our ideas come out of joint struggle rather than being any one individual's property.

This book nevertheless owes a particular debt to three people: Colin Barker, who patiently and through his own extraordinary intellectual example showed me how to think dialectically about social movements; Alf Nilsen, with whom I have collaborated for over two decades on the approach that underpins many of the arguments here (and which is more explicit in our joint *We Make Our Own History: Marxism and Social Movements in the Twilight of Neoliberalism*); and Geoffrey Pleyers, whose project 'Social movements in a global age' made it possible for me to visit the Fondation maison des sciences de l'homme/Collège d'études mondiales in Paris, where this book was written. I am very grateful to the Collège for providing a kind of intellectual space which is all too rare.

Very many thanks to 'Anastasia' and 'Pat' for letting me share part of their stories in chapter 1 (Seán is a composite). And many thanks to Alf, Geoffrey, Órfhlaith Tuohy and Tomás MacSheoin, who all took the time to read and comment patiently on an earlier version of this book. Its weaknesses are all mine.

I also need to make an apology to readers: no one can be involved in all movements, live in all places or know all histories equally well. We have an obligation to take each other's existence seriously, but it is a form of naïve positivism to assume that we should all read everything each other has written or familiarise ourselves with each other's culture. Linguistically, we are all constrained by the number of languages that we can reasonably learn to an effective level. So little is translated into English that we have to assume, and gesture at, the existence of whole political and intellectual conversations of which an Anglophone monoglot can only access a small, and often very selective, fragment. By analogy, the same is true for different movements (whose reflections in intellectual journals often privilege certain kinds of celebrity), but also for different academic disciplines and political traditions. We have to speak from where we are, but in an attempt to speak to one another out of this particular experience.

This book is 'Eurocentric' in the concrete sense that it is written by a west European with several local languages but few language skills outside that space, only limited historical knowledge outside it (primarily in relation to Buddhist Asia) and involved in movements here, with their specific sets of international solidarities and alliances rather than others. In my own work I try to draw on this experience critically – including its shaping by colonial relationships, which are also fundamental to understanding Ireland – and to credit the rest of the world with equal complexity and equal depths, resisting superficial hand-waving as far as possible. This book is also shaped by the history of my involvement with a particular kind of social movement left, with specific movements and with the dialogues they represent: nobody can be involved in everything, even in a single city. This book talks more about the things I know in concrete ways, but the test of the arguments made here is not in relation to the examples they use but rather in how well they work in other contexts.

Since capitalism's latest crash a decade ago, the combination of austerity-induced cuts to real wages, my partner's disability and unemployment and the attempt to find alternative education for my daughter has meant that it has been a constant struggle to get through to the end of the month. I am more grateful than words can express to the friends and family, colleagues and companer@s who have helped us keep our heads above water, especially when they have not agreed with our choices but have helped us anyway. You know who you are: this book is dedicated to you.

Chapter 1

Why We Need Social Movements

Anastasia (not her real name) has a son on the autistic spectrum. To access any kind of resources for him, she had to wait four years to get an official diagnosis, by which point her son was already six. The waiting lists for assessments are so long that another parent with a special needs child set up a private centre with subsidised rates so that parents can know what their children need – while they are still children. Her then partner had to take a case with the ombudsman in order to get minimal treatment from inexperienced staff, and go through a lengthy appeal process in order to be entitled to carer's leave. They now have to fight with the school and the teacher to get them to take their son's condition at all seriously in daily classroom work. Despite having to pursue this route, Anastasia does not feel that the official psychiatric diagnosis, or the practices in which their son's special needs assistant have been trained, really describe or help his situation very well; and she has deep-seated questions about how and why he is on the spectrum – but also why school and society are organised in such a way that it is excruciatingly difficult for autistic people to function within them. After all, school supports will mostly cease in children's teens or at best early adulthood; and all being well children outlive their parents. How are they to survive? With other parents, she has set up a local group which provides supports to parents and carers and helps people fill out welfare forms and campaigns for changes in the system: the local health board now refers parents with autism to them rather than changing its own practice. Because of her own health situation Anastasia is limited in her energy, but she also holds down two part-time jobs, in a community centre and an alternative school project.

Seán is a 'nice boy from a good family', but never really fitted into the macho world around him, partly because his parents were immigrants and partly because he was attracted to men as well as women. From an early age, he read intensively and in his teenage years became deeply affected by the suffering and injustice in the world. In his personal life, but also his work as a mental health nurse, he tries to act in ways that take all of this on board – challenging sexist and racist stereotypes among his colleagues, not eating animals, helping organise the local union branch – while also joining in more political actions when he can, from antiwar politics as a student to involvement in local food projects as an adult. In the small town where he now lives in another country, there is a real crisis situation around undocumented migrants, racist organising and Syrian refugees. Seán tries not only to help organise welcome and support structures as well as language classes for the newcomers, but also to develop anti-racist activities for local working-class youth.

Pat came from a very difficult family background and struggled to bring her sons up on a working-class estate without them falling victim to addiction or the police. She is a resourceful woman: when her sons' friends were hanging around the alleyway behind her house smoking dope, she used her comfortable 'mammy' persona to invite them in for a cup of tea. As teenage lads, they didn't quite know what to do except to come in and look embarrassed. Over the years she gradually won their confidence, not lecturing them about what they should be doing but listening as they talked about the lack of any obvious future; the way teachers, shopkeepers and respectable citizens treated them; harassment by the police; and the deaths of their friends by suicide or overdose. Slowly but surely she helped them to reflect more on the power relations underlying this situation, and as they did so they also found it easier to take charge of their own lives in many ways. She now spends a lot of time working with women's groups from council estates like her own, helping them think more about how society is organised and how they can improve things locally. She supported her daughter in her many battles with school authorities and is delighted that she calls herself a feminist.

MOVEMENTS ARE EVERYDAY THINGS

I could multiply these examples indefinitely, but these three snapshots give something of the sense of the down-to-earth and everyday nature of most social movement organising. In fact it is so down-to-earth that people involved often refuse the label of 'activist' and strongly resist the idea that they are doing anything special or different. Just like those around them, they say, they try to help when they can.

Indeed, they are likely to feel that they cannot do enough to respond to all the suffering they are conscious of, and this points to something important: few people are full-time, lifelong organisers. It is very common to dip in and out of different movements and activism (a word I use for lack of a better one) throughout people's whole lives. This is just as well: otherwise, movements would consist of the same handful of people, with probably very little resonance in workplaces or communities. Instead, sometimes – by no means all the time – people feel strongly enough, or strongly affected enough, about a particular issue or campaign that they decide to get involved, whether or not they have done so before.

Total newcomers often bring a great blast of energy and confidence, and a refreshing lack of awareness that some areas or groups may be hostile to movements, and these can be huge strengths. As Facebook groups previously devoted to gossiping about each other start sharing videos of police violence, or as friends or neighbours turning out for a march on an issue they are outraged about take a week to produce a brilliant banner together, there is a great jolt of life for movements and longer-term organisers.

But whether we are first-time participants, long-time organisers, occasional participants or for that matter observers keeping our distance, as soon as you start looking you see that social movements are everywhere. Not all the time, certainly, and not equally successful. This is part of what defines 'normality': since movements come together in part to challenge the way things are, 'normality' means precisely those times and places in which the social institutions and routines that suit the powerful, the wealthy and the culturally privileged are not significantly challenged. Even in periods of utter normality, however, people still come together to fight where they have to – to protect their children, in their workplaces or communities; and other people still resist injustice, whether official support for wars and dictatorship abroad or ecological destruction at home, even when they have little hope of success.

A lot of this activity is very mundane: the support group, the leaflet, the website, the Twitter argument, the invitation to a new colleague to join the union, the small local demonstration to defend services, the email to politicians or the subscription to an NGO. Because social movements are everywhere, they are 'nothing special'; or rather, only some of the time do we even really notice movement activity as out of the ordinary. They go beyond charity in that they have some degree of self-organisation – they are not simply created by the state, local businesses, a church or a committee of local 'notables' – and this is partly because they ask bigger questions about the world and go that bit further, in their ideas even if not always in their action (which is harder to achieve).

SOCIAL MOVEMENTS AND HUMAN NEEDS

To outline a more formal way of thinking about social movements: Human beings, all of us, have needs, all sorts of them – for food and for hope, for ideas and for love, for health care and for respect, for shelter and for real work, needs for our children and for the place we live in and so on. When we meet one need, we see that there are other things we also need – or, sometimes, when one need is met, we realise that we need not just shelter but *decent* shelter, whether in terms of cost, quality or how the landlord treats us. Needs, in other words, are developmental, not fixed and given. This is not only true for us as individuals but also at a cultural or social level – what an older generation was not much bothered by can be really distressing to us. We are often aware of needs that aren't fully met, while sometimes we are taken by surprise to discover how much we needed something once we get a small taste of it. This is incidentally often true of meaningful involvement in social struggle around things that really matter to us.

At one level, social inequality is about how far these needs are met; and in capitalist societies, we are offered an 'equality of opportunity' in which we are invited to compete to see if our needs can be met. Of course, this usually means that other people's needs are not, or not met as much; and we may be very well aware that some of the things that are most important to us are never in practice going to be made available to us, that they are basically reserved to other categories of people.

At another level, our kinds of society – based on divisions of class, of gender and sexuality, of race and ethnicity, with states and cultures that support these divisions – are only really interested in a narrow subset of human needs. Hence, even what is offered to 'successful' people is often very short on some of the things that we might feel make life most worthwhile – free time, for example, real human community, a wide natural world within which to wander freely, social equality, a deeper sense of meaning, participation in the decisions that affect us or even the ability to live well without feeling that other people are suffering and dying elsewhere for our benefit. So in order to keep going, our kinds of society offer to selectively meet our needs, in ways conditional on our behaving appropriately, often at the expense of others and with certain needs ruled right out; and many of us know full well that our most urgent needs are simply not going to be met.

We are not, of course, going to stop trying to meet our needs, one way or the other. If we can meet them within the everyday routines and practices we are offered, we are quite likely to try to do so. We are also quite likely to try and meet other needs in unofficial ways when this is the easiest thing to do: an informal arrangement about when we leave work, swapping childcare or school lifts, a bit of dope to help us calm down, watching pirated movies or asking family members for help. A lot of the time, though, none of this quite does it for us. We do not get to the end of the month without borrowing money or leaving bills unopened for fear of what they might say; we hate our job; our living situation is driving us demented; our child is miserable and none of the approved channels are helping; every time we turn on the TV we get furious at the world we see out there.

So we struggle to cope in everyday life; and at times we feel we have things under control, at times we do not. Sometimes, though, we sense the possibility of pushing things further: changing how a particular institution works, at least at a small level; setting up a new project that would do things better and differently; coming together with people more like ourselves to do the things we value, even when they are illegal or frowned upon. At other times, we feel definitely under attack: we come together to try to defend services that we badly need, to stop a cut in wages or make sure permanent jobs are not turned into contract ones, to express our outrage and try to stop a war, an appalling political leader or the destruction of the planet. Movements are a creative collective response to this sort of situation.

Chapter 4 talks more about this process theoretically; here I want to underline that *because* we have human needs, and *because* our societies only meet those partially and for some of us, it is common enough to come together collectively to try to do something about this: to resist, or to push forward; to create new institutions or new forms of socialising; even at times to imagine a different and better world – or to try to stop a worse one which seems to be almost upon us.

MOVEMENTS AND OUR OWN LIVES

We are not always available to do this, or only in certain ways. Social movement researchers talk about this as biographical availability. For example, my child and partner (who has an invisible disability) live elsewhere in order to meet their particular needs, and as the only person in well-paid employment I have to concentrate on making money in order to keep this whole show on the road financially, while my partner does most of the care work and only gets a respite at weekends when I am there. Under these circumstances, I will not be going to many Saturday demos for a good few years, and my involvement in other kinds of activism will be severely limited by my ability to follow through on organising commitments. So too with other kinds of caring and work responsibilities, with our own disabilities, sickness or old age or when we are particularly vulnerable to certain kinds of reprisals, like police violence or losing our job.

There may be other kinds of situational barriers to participation. We may only have encountered kinds of activism that didn't seem to have any place for people like us, or that seemed to depend on following people we didn't really like or respect; we might have moved into a situation where there seems no prospect of involving other people in the kinds of things we care about; or we might already be under a cloud of suspicion for being too different in one way or another. Some of these things, maybe, can be worked around – there are often ways of getting people on your side if the right situation arises or you are able to think creatively; or there may be forms of activism that can be carried out with the time and energy we actually have available. But at other times, movement participation may simply not be on the cards.

Thus many people weave in and out of movements as their lives change. The reason why there is a stereotype of the college activist is in part because this is one of the times of life in which we are most likely to encounter our peers engaging in activism and recognise it as such, but it is by no means the only one. In fact, there are many different spaces of social movement. Some, like trade union activism, are structured around where we work; others, such as community activism and some kinds of environmental or service protest, are very much structured around where we live. Some take place in our 'leisure time', in that they happen after work, online or at weekends in largely public spaces, and may bring together people from all sorts of social situations; some exist primarily *as* a job, in the sense of a Greenpeace worker, a radical journalist or a staff member in a women's refuge. At times, as in the US mobilisation against Trump, we see people resisting across all of these spaces: resigning their jobs, or carrying them out in ways that actively frustrate administration plans; taking whole school districts out on strike, or mobilising at the airport to welcome Muslims and resist the travel ban; pushing to defend and strengthen the sanctuary status of particular cities or campuses; organising on a neighbourhood basis to resist raids for undocumented migrants; supporting each other in the workplace; and so on.

Not only are we likely to encounter movements in different spaces of our lives; our lives are likely to intersect with them in very different ways. To take a strong example, in some times and spaces – Zapatista communities in Chiapas today or some republican communities in Northern Ireland during the Troubles – most people might be in some sense involved in activism, in different ways at different times in their lives of course, but with no sense that to do so is anything other than normal. A certain level of feminist activism may work like this at the moment in some social groups, meaning that 'my daughter just announced that she is a feminist' is an ordinary statement which friends and family meet with rejoicing as a normal part of growing up.

A more common situation is that of a lifeworld where a particular movement is broadly accepted and taking part in it is nothing unusual or remarkable, although many people do not take part, or only in limited ways. This has been the case for lesbian and gay communities in many cities for some decades, and for politically organised working-class communities in much of the global North until fairly recently. In these situations, most people may turn out to

Pride for the party, or (when working) are largely inactive union members, and know some of the songs, while being more or less supportive of actual actions and campaigns. There might be tensions around how people in some organisations treat those who aren't, and a certain amount of joking as between those who prefer to watch the match and those who prefer to go to a meeting, but being an activist is not a problem in itself; it is a relatively well-understood way of being, and there are many supports available for learning the part.

These kinds of situations – as the examples given above suggest – are historically created; they come and go. Often, this means that there are sharp generational barriers so that (for example) the parents of young blacks who became involved in the Civil Rights Movement might have been proud of them but at the same time scared for them, and tried to dissuade them from placing themselves at risk. The parents of young ecologists in the 1980s might have had furious arguments with them about meat-eating or driving two cars. More sharply, German students in the 1960s started to ask their parents about what they had done 'in the war'. These first generations are often shaped in lifelong ways by this break from the culture they grew up in – while their peers made other choices with far more deeply conservative meanings, in a time when the best and the brightest were rejecting the world that the more cynical or the less creative were trying to slot into.

Last, some movements take place on the edge of their social; these can thus be hardest to sustain at a personal level. This is very often true for culturally radical movements, from animal rights to new religious movements; for the far left in countries where it is a marginal force; and for movements structured around creating new kinds of institutions, such as organic farms, urban social centres, radical education projects or cooperatives. There are simply not many models in society for how to live like this, and often little understanding to be had from friends or family. This can easily mean that participants become particularly dependent on movement institutions in terms of how they live their lives, and face particular challenges as the movement changes or if they break with other participants.

Of course in some ways each of these situations is an extreme case. More commonly, everyday life in most contemporary cultures involves *some* acceptance of *some* kind of movement participation as reasonable and normal, whether that means community education in a working-class estate, resisting gentrification in a lively inner-city area, organising against environmentally destructive projects in 'unspoilt' rural areas, mobilising to defend welfare services, setting up a carpool or childcare project, multicultural initiatives to welcome refugees or volunteering on a domestic violence helpline. In fact part of the battle that movements fight is precisely around how to achieve this level of cultural acceptance *without* this meaning depoliticisation, becoming a lifestyle activity or purely selfish in nature.

WHAT WE MEET IN MOVEMENTS,
AND WHAT WE FIND IN OURSELVES

Negative impressions of social movements are best countered by actually spending time with real activists (rather than media caricatures) and seeing what their lives are like. To take an unusual example: for many years, I have worked with people involved in the Waldorf school movement inspired by Rudolf Steiner and have come to know people involved in the Camphill residential communities for people with special needs, in biodynamic farming and in the Ruskin Mill project which uses craft as therapy for young adults with special needs – all Steiner-linked and associated with anthroposophy, the spiritual movement he founded. I am not an anthroposophist in any way and find many of the ideas proposed by Steiner hard to swallow; and there is room for serious debate around some of the practices of the different movements mentioned above, debate which some of their participants join in.

Yet what stands out for me from this experience is meeting people who dedicate their lives over many years to enormously demanding and difficult projects: sustaining alternative schools, where teachers with high levels of training and experience often earn salaries a fraction of what they could earn in the mainstream; bringing people with special needs into one's own family, and thus acting as voluntary lifelong carers as well as friends and parents; seeing one project after another fail and having to move (often to another country) and try to start again; and facing a barrage of challenges ranging from state hostility through the financial challenges of keeping these kinds of services going, to personal attacks.

These are not easy experiences, and yet the people I know usually manage to encounter the world with a great calm, a real interest in the people they meet and a great kindness towards people with special needs, children or young adults with sometimes threatening behavioural issues. There is a real love of beauty to be found in their workplaces – often at the cost of working far past the time when anyone else would have gone home – a fascination with ideas, and a deep ethical practice.

Look below the issue, or the ideas, in other words – and here I have deliberately chosen examples which most people are unfamiliar with or hostile to – and you find that social movement participants are often people who look beyond themselves, both on an interpersonal level and intellectually; people who are more concerned with benefitting others than with serving themselves; and people with great staying power and a real love for the world and other people, even when this is sometimes expressed negatively and critically, in outrage at injustice.

The details, and the ways people live with themselves and their work, differ hugely between movements: but the basic point is as true for solidarity and development workers as for socialist activists, for people in NGOs delivering services as for unpaid community activists, for trade unionists as for anti-racist organisers, for disability rights activists as for feminists: their human qualities are often deeply impressive. Whether it is these qualities that have brought them to activism, or that activism has encouraged these qualities, is perhaps a chicken-and-egg question. I do not want to suggest for a minute that all activists are saints: anyone familiar with movements will know that there are some common failings (not least self-righteousness) and some individuals who are just hard work to deal with – though it might be worth considering what such people would be like if they were not making the efforts involved in activism. . .

There *is* a real human difference that comes with long-term dedication to something that goes beyond yourself and your immediate family (even if it starts there); that involves thinking about the world in deeper ways and not simply taking the simplest set of clichés for granted; that often involves dropping your immediate activity in order to help someone in a crisis; and that involves putting yourself at risk, or losing out financially, or risking mockery and contempt, for some bigger purpose.

Of course in many cultures there are broader senses of generosity and mutual aid, hospitality and help in a crisis, sharing and neighbourly responsibilities that are not restricted to activists. These are, after all, strong parts of what might be said to constitute decent human existence. It could reasonably be argued that in the more individualised worlds which neoliberal capitalism in particular tries to create and celebrate, where we are encouraged not to feel responsible for other people's suffering or to even see other people *as* people, activism keeps these positive human qualities alive, or gives them a new kind of lease of life in a hostile setting; while other people only resist by remaining decent and generous in their private lives but not beyond this.

And as we see in moments like recent outpourings of popular generosity in response to the Syrian refugee crisis, or of courage in resistance to racism, the qualities neoliberalism seeks to squash pop up again despite everything, even when as in Europe today they then struggle to find a more organised expression. Part of the human value of social movements, then, is to put these qualities on a stronger footing against the conscious organisation of greed and self-centred isolationism, hate and stupidity as political forces. Some of the best writing from movements has an aesthetic which recognises both the concrete grimness of the world and these extraordinary qualities, expressed in people's visions of and struggles for a better world.

REMAKING OURSELVES IN MOVEMENTS

In this chapter, I have tried to give a sense of social movements as not being so strange, but as something we may well have participated in at some point in our lives, or even be involved in at present without thinking of it like this. I have looked at some aspects of how people live with their own movement participation, whether occasional or otherwise; and I have said something about how being in movements can affect people for the better. Movements, then, are close at hand, not as alien and distant as their opponents would like us to think; and this is a crucial political fact.

We started by exploring how people become involved in movements in order to meet their own needs and those of others; and having arrived at the human qualities of activists, I want to return to the question of how movement participation benefits us, in ways that also benefit others. Movement participation itself, of course, meets *some* needs, in the process of trying to meet others; and this is really important for understanding how people can keep going in the face of external defeat.

At a trivial level, it is of course not uncommon to join movements in order to make friends, because we have fallen in love with someone, or because we want to make a statement; and movements can give us something to do, a way of feeling that our lives have meaning, and a new kind of friendship and community. None of these are bad things; we could find some or many of them in other kinds of group setting, because as human beings we do actually need each other. Whether family or colleagues, neighbours or friends, it is hard to live without other people (even in the literal sense of life expectancy). It is no bad thing to meet these needs in a way that also benefits people beyond ourselves.

At a deeper level, and one which is not available in many other contexts, movements are a form of collective self-creation, and this meets some really powerful human needs. We are always, to some extent, remaking ourselves, consciously or unconsciously. All too often we are trying to remake ourselves in line with forces outside ourselves: bombarded by advertising, we try to make ourselves more attractive; under pressure at work, we try to make ourselves more competitive; struggling to make connections, we try to fit in. Social movements mean questioning some of those forces (usually not all, or not all at once).

Movements involve, it could be said, a process of education and emancipation: education in terms of thinking more deeply about different kinds of social relationship, power structure or cultural norms – and emancipation in the sense of taking practical action around this. This practical action, even in small doses, is transformative and contrasts sharply with letting our everyday actions be driven by habit while relating to the world through opinions alone. As we try to convince our neighbour to come to a meeting, or challenge our local authority, or try to make a kindergarten project work, we are exploring the practical meaning of our ideas and changing our ideas in line with our experience.

We are educating ourselves, not in isolation as one might do with an obsessive reading habit, or in a top-down way as one can do at college within an existing discipline, but in a genuinely adult way, not one set up by someone else, and where what other people do and say is central to our learning process and not fully predictable or within our control; in fact this is almost defining of the social movement experience. We are much more fully present in the learning situation, both with respect to other movement participants and with respect to opponents and the not yet committed. There is a collective, interactive and conflictual aspect to our learning.

This self-creation, in the Marxist tradition, is labelled as 'praxis', nominally the unity of (intellectual) theory and (political) practice – though I think it is less a fixed unity and a bit more like riding a bicycle: as we articulate our ideas, we come to try them out in the world; as things go wrong (or better than expected), we change our ideas and as all of this happens, we grow and develop, come into ourselves more fully in this relationship with other people.

A WARM EVENING IN DUBLIN

Another way of putting this is to say that social movements represent the practice of what activists are increasingly calling real democracy: popular power that goes beyond ticking a box once every few years and otherwise accepting the power of authority in the state, of employers in the workplace or of 'the way we do things' in the rest of our lives. In movements, we learn to self-organise and take decisions democratically about the things that affect us, whether in an alternative project or in conflict with powerful opponents.

These very conflicts are where we find out just how much we can assert control over our own lives. In May 2004, I was one of the media spokespeople for a 'weekend for an alternative Europe', protesting as Ireland hosted an EU summit. We argued that the EU was becoming defined by the deaths of migrants struggling to enter a new 'Fortress Europe'; that it was increasingly a military actor, overriding Irish neutrality; that EU policies were transferring the weight of taxation from the rich to the poor and privatising public services and more generally that the EU was enshrining neoliberal economics and top-down decision-making.

In response to these, we wanted to make the experiment of seeing if it was possible, in an EU then still celebrated as a bastion of democracy, to have our voices literally heard by EU leaders: could we come close enough that they could hear our protest? It turned out that the threat of being embarrassed in front of the EU worried the Irish government enough that it called out the military as well as the police. Scare stories leaked to the media accused us of having arms dumps and planning gas attacks (obviously, we didn't); attempts were made to frighten city-centre shopkeepers into rolling down the shutters for the weekend; the media were informed that our march had been called off; and the riot squad were drafted in to prevent us assembling. All this for a peaceful march whose biggest risk was that banging pots and pans (a form of protest borrowed from Argentina) might be noisy enough that the leaders' banquet would be disturbed.

But rights and liberties are not granted from on high; they are taken from below. It is not up to the government, or the police, to decide whether or not we can protest; it is up to us as human beings to assert the right to assemble and the right to protest, in practice. In the event, it turned out that so many other people cared about these rights that the march was several times the size it might otherwise have been, and we got well within shouting (or rather pot-banging) distance of the banquet before being turned back by water cannon and baton charges. It was possible to express our dissent, in other words, if we were well-organised.

It was a long evening for me; I later calculated that I had walked fourteen kilometres in a few hours, going backwards and forwards trying to keep the march from being separated into sections that could be broken up by the police. The most powerful experience of the event, for me, was being part of a large insurgent crowd calling 'Whose streets? Our streets!' The streets do not belong to the police, even if they beat us off them; they do not belong to the government, to close any time it is politically inconvenient that people protest; they belong to the people. But for the streets to become our streets *in practice*, we have to take them back, together. In a similar way, decades previously, feminists organised 'Take Back the Night' marches against sexual violence in public spaces. The practice of democracy consists of these moments of popular self-assertion, finding out if we agree that certain things (banning marches, sexual violence) are unacceptable, seeing the nature of the opposition (the state, patriarchy), and acting on that together, to reshape our world.

RECONNECTION

In a world where what psychologist Oliver James has called affluenza, the disease of isolated individual consumption, has become rampant, and where Asperger syndrome has become so widespread that it has been removed even from the conservative psychiatric DSM-5 manual, such reconnection is an urgent need for many of us. Movements enable this reconnection not simply within the protected space of a stable, routine and predictable institution but through meeting one another as comrades in the struggle or as opponents, as allies to be convinced or as uncommitted people to engage with – and in ask-ing real questions about the situation we are in, whose interests it serves, how it has come to be and what it might take to change it.

In this sense, movements also offer the possibility of growing into a level of adulthood which is rare in the present world, a full and first-person engagement with our social reality not simply through coping or cynicism but through collective and creative action. There is a sort of childishness in a depoliticised way of life which simply accepts all the human-created struc-tures of the world around us as given and unchangeable, and restricts itself to grumbling about this and cheerleading for that. In most human societies, for most of our species' existence, *making* our own world – in the very practi-cal sense of constructing shelter, making clothes and tools, creating art and social rituals and, since the Neolithic, farming – has been a central part of the human experience.

Marxists have long observed that capitalism alienates us more and more from this experience. It is noticeable how important things like garden-ing, making music, cooking, home improvements, organising social events and other attempts to create at least part of our own world are to so many people – even at the same time as these things are alienated again and turned into opportunities for consumption, improvement of house values, spectator sports or status displays. Social movement action is about stepping back into the real space of making our world on the widest scale; when we are invited to a gay wedding, see our children organise for women's rights with no fear or self-consciousness, enjoy the weekend, watch politicians back off from an unpopular measure, meet South Africans who have grown up after apartheid or see new kinds of school appear on the horizon, there is a sharp reminder of how much we have actually changed our world through collective struggle.

Chapter 2

Movements Made
the World We Live In

When injustice, inequality, oppression or exploitation are substantial and long-lasting, it is a fair bet that they are not accidental. People tend not just to notice such things but also, as we have seen, to try and change them. Homelessness, violence against women, global poverty, racism, climate change and so on provoke a normal human response, not just once but repeatedly. If calls for change consistently fall on deaf ears and attempts to bring about change are consistently blocked, it is not credible to imagine that somehow the powerful, the wealthy and the culturally privileged simply haven't noticed – however comforting that belief might be.

More typically, and more realistically, oppressive power structures persist because they suit the powerful. Exploitation persists because the wealthy benefit; and cultural stigmatisation persists because those at the top of the hierarchy quite like it that way. And, of course, the wealthy, the powerful and the culturally privileged tend to overlap significantly, and to support one another when they are not (as they often are) actually the same people. *Ending* injustice, then, is typically an uphill battle against these groups, and the institutions and social routines they dominate, such as the state, capital, patriarchy or racism. For the substantial and long-lasting forms of injustice we are discussing here, such battles are typically themselves both hard and long, fought by the much greater numbers of the poor, the powerless and the culturally stigmatised, or at least by a significant proportion of them.

Take an obvious example: winning the vote. The history is different in different countries, but the vast majority of states were not democracies in any sense until recently but more or less absolute monarchies, imperial colonies or dictatorships of various kinds. Few kings, imperial powers or dictators have ever relinquished power voluntarily. The explosive threat posed by popular power is shown by the consistency with which the history of the vote is marked by restricted suffrage (to men only, with a property qualification, over a certain age, to a limited group of citizens and so on), by limited powers given to elected bodies (as against the monarch, the imperial centre, the military and so on) and by complicated arrangements (presidents vs. parliaments, upper vs. lower houses, courts vs. parliaments etc.) designed to restrict the possible implications of popular decisions. It was not until the mid-twentieth century in most countries that 'democrat' ceased to be a term of abuse, with meanings between 'anarchy' and 'mob rule'.

In fact, however, the violence was typically on the other foot. In 1819, when the vote was restricted to only a small fraction of the population, a huge meeting in Manchester demanding electoral reform was met by the cavalry, the artillery and the militia. Perhaps a dozen people were killed and several hundred injured at what became known as 'Peterloo'. A limited reform in 1832 extended voting rights to some middle class men only. Between 1838 and the 1850s Britain's Chartist movement, one of the first mass working-class movements, organised huge numbers of supporters around six demands: a vote for all men over twenty-one, the secret ballot, no property qualification for members of parliament, payment for members (so people without private incomes could stand for parliament), equal-sized constituencies and annual parliamentary elections to ensure popular control over parliament.

Some of the Chartists' demands, 180 years old this year, are still short of being met. Annual elections are still absent everywhere, while constituency gerrymandering remains a fine art in many jurisdictions, not least the US. Recall that a civil war was fought over slavery, and the right to vote for most black men was only technically granted after the war. This was immediately contested in practice, both by the violence of the Ku Klux Klan and other racist organisations and by a wide range of bureaucratic rules designed to disenfranchise blacks. The Civil Rights Movement of the 1950s and 1960s faced lethal violence in the struggle to enforce the right to vote; in today's US, attempts to restrict the black vote remain a battleground in many states.

In the Britain, the great Chartist demonstration of 1848 has been described as the nearest the country came to revolution; another two limited reforms, a radical women's suffrage movement and mass labour organising, followed. Despite this, it was not until 1918 that all men over twenty-one were given the right to vote; women over thirty who met a property qualification were also included, with equal suffrage granted in 1928. Britain has thus only been a democracy in any real sense for ninety years – and it took ninety years of radical struggle to get to that point. In Northern Ireland, the demand for equal voting rights in regional and local government provoked violent responses from loyalist mobs, with de facto police support. By the time local government was reformed, in 1973, the regional government had been suspended and Northern Ireland was run from Westminster with military support.

With all its limitations, universal suffrage was not handed down by benevolent rulers or the product of some magical law of progress: it was fought for and won by large-scale, radical social movements against consistent and often lethal resistance from those in power.

SEEING THE BIGGER PICTURE

So too in many other ways, social movements have made the world we live in – not, as Marx observed, under circumstances of their own choosing; and not all outcomes of social movements were the ones they wanted or the ones we might celebrate. Nonetheless, a sober reckoning of *just how far* the world we live in is the product of collective struggle is a necessary starting point for understanding our own world and the effects of our own past actions, to think through how we remake it in our present struggles, and to see more clearly what it means to be human.

Chapter 1 explored this dynamic from an individual perspective. In this chapter, I want to pull back to a far larger collective, historical and global perspective in order to look at the other side of this. The need for a bigger picture is a real human one, readily visible in any bookshop in the form of 'key to the universe' books which offer to explain everything in history and the present world in terms of economics, or genetics; through diseases, or ideas; as psychology, or as geopolitics. Clearly, the question 'how can we understand our world?' bubbles up time and time again; equally clearly, there is a strong ideological push to answer this question in ways that not only 'sell' a particular academic discipline but also give us the sense of seeing 'under' the surface of reality that other people take for granted. This chapter does not attempt to offer such a key to the universe or a special secret: it is mostly a reminder of familiar historical facts, which are so big we tend to take them for granted, and an encouragement to think about them more systematically.

For the past quarter-millennium, the world has seen one wave of social movements after another, each challenging and in some cases dramatically reshaping some aspect of what Immanuel Wallerstein calls the capitalist world-system. A good place to start the story is with the 'Atlantic Revolutions' of the later eighteenth century that challenged the world of the triangle trade (slaves, cotton and textiles between Africa, America and Europe). The successful American and French Revolutions provided models of state organisation, as well as narratives of popular uprising, that remain immensely powerful nearly 250 years later, while Haiti saw the first successful revolution against slavery (1791–1804) and 1798 in Ireland marks a large-scale uprising close to the heart of British power. Parliamentary government, and the end of empires, have long roots in popular resistance.

The early nineteenth century saw a wave of revolutionary wars bring most of today's Latin American nation-states into being, from Mexico to Chile, while the European movements of 1848 shook the old dynastic order to the core in the name of radical-democratic nationalism, 'the people' defined in national and cultural terms against states structured in terms of monarchic ruling houses. This model of what 'a country' is has subsequently become so widespread that it is hardly possible to escape from it anywhere on the planet today.

In 1915/1916 the opening shots were fired in a process that would see the end of the empires that then covered almost the entire Old World (with the exception of Tibet, Thailand, Japan and to some extent China). The transnational Ghadar movement brought together Bengali and Punjabi labour migrants to North America with radical Indian nationalist intellectuals in a failed attempt at achieving independence through a mutiny in the British Indian Army. The Easter Rising in my own city of Dublin started a process that led within a few years to the withdrawal of the British Empire from most of its closest neighbour. Finally, the Zimmerwald meeting in neutral Switzerland brought together the radical wing of European social democracy, those opposed to nationalist warfare and in favour of socialist internationalism: the foundations of the communist traditions that shook the twentieth-century world.

The wave of popular struggles that followed fatally undermined the war effort, as workers went on strike and peasants occupied the land across much of Europe, while most of the belligerent armies were crippled by mutinies and desertions. Workers', peasants', soldiers' and sailors' councils (sometimes using the Russian word, *soviet*) flourished across the continent. The few liberal parliamentary states of the period suffered massive labour unrest, with a general strike in Seattle and the US' Red Scare targeting labour activists, socialists and anarchists, while troops were sent onto the streets of Liverpool, Glasgow and Belfast. Italy's 'two red years' saw factory occupations across its northern industrial cities and a huge wave of land occupations.

Across the continent, the dynastic empires of 1914 were broken apart by a surge of radical left movements of different kinds, not only in Russia but also with the Hungarian Soviet and 'Red Vienna' in what had been Austro-Hungary. In Germany, a series of revolutionary conflicts brought down the Kaiser, creating and then contesting the Weimar Republic. Finally, Europe's internal colonies rebelled, from Ireland to Finland and Poland. This wave was beaten back in various ways, with the Irish Free State and the USSR the only surviving remnants of its most revolutionary edge, both having lost significant territory and facing civil war as well as – for the USSR – intervention by a dozen Allied powers. In the bigger picture, however, the Hohenzollern, Romanov, Hapsburg and Ottoman empires were swept away, never to return.

This wave was partly contained by a new kind of violence: paramilitary forces drawing on the minority of ex-soldiers who wanted to keep on fighting, for reasons of class and ideology, because of personal trauma or psychopathology, or because they had nothing else to go back to. In Italy, the armed gangs associated with the Fascist Party were supported by business interests and big landowners to attack labour and socialist organisers and break up land occupations. In Germany, the newly established Weimar Republic made a 'pact with the devil' of the right-wing paramilitary *Freikorps* and the police and military establishments to defend it against challenges from the left; this rendered the new republic fatally dependent on forces that were ultimately hostile to it. In Ireland, the 'Black and Tan' police reserves, recruited on a similar basis, were successful in provoking popular hostility, burning several towns, but could not prevent partial independence.

LEFT AND RIGHT AFTER 1919

The European 'civil war', over what was to replace the old order, ran through the birth of right-wing states in Italy, Hungary and Germany over the corpses of their defeated opponents. A similar struggle would happen in Spain from 1936 to 1939 as an elected left-wing government faced a military uprising under Franco. The combination of German military power and local right-wing forces in various kinds of collaborationist arrangement would expand fascist power up until the decisive battle of Stalingrad in 1942, when the Red Army started to turn the tide.

After Stalingrad, with the growth of labour conscription in occupied Europe and the opening of new fronts in Italy and eventually France, large-scale popular resistance to fascism grew. These new recruits joined the longer resistance of anarchists, communists, socialists and trade unionists against a regime bent on their annihilation, as well as (in different countries) radical democrats, right-wing nationalists opposed to German rule, Jewish partisans and others. The Yalta settlement, dividing the postwar continent between the two emerging superpowers and Britain, was superimposed on this conflict, and contested memories of collaboration, resistance and liberation remain central to debates over state legitimacy today, which can be read in military terms as a conflict between nations or in political terms as a conflict between left and right.

While fascist Spain and Portugal, which had remained neutral in the war, preserved their arrangements until the mid-1970s, welfare states in the US-dominated west and state socialisms in the Soviet-dominated east both attempted in different ways to satisfy popular demands while maintaining their superpowers' preferred forms of state power and economic structure. Both saw processes of economic redistribution as well as a 'social wage' in the form of education, health, housing, welfare and so on, with political structures that supposedly enabled the mediation of hierarchically organised economic interests at a central level. These states were nonetheless contested, most dramatically by the US Civil Rights Movement from the mid-1950s on and by working-class uprisings in East Germany (1953) and Hungary (1956).

With the end of war in Asia came a new wave of national liberation movements. These had been forged under British, French and Dutch colonial domination and reshaped in response to the expansion of Japan's 'Greater East Asia Co-Prosperity Sphere'. The military collapse of European empires in 1941 combined with the growth of popular anti-colonial movements to make new states so clearly inevitable that the British Empire began negotiating its withdrawal almost immediately after the war. The French resisted in Indochina, and were defeated in 1954 at Dien Bien Phu but replaced by the Americans; the Vietnam war did not end until 1975.

The constellations of movements underlying the new states varied hugely, with different relationships between peasant struggles, urban working-class organisation and the new educated elites, and in the relative weight of nationalism, socialism and religion as political projects around which people could envisage their future struggles around modernity. The difference between the new Chinese and Indian states, widely discussed up to the 1970s, is telling in this respect.

African anti-colonial movements in the 1950s and 1960s also went through a combination of fighting their way to independence (most dramatically in Kenya and Algeria) and negotiated colonial withdrawal. Here popular movements were often weaker than in Asia, and precolonial state structures contributed less to the shape of empire and the borders which followed. Here too, long anti-colonial struggles had to be fought, notably in Angola, Rhodesia and South Africa (this last finishing only in 1994).

This second anti-colonial wave (after the end of empire in the Americas) was both long-lasting in its effects and ambiguous. Almost everywhere, these new states – whether officially communist, nationalist, religious or some combination of these – attempted 'national-developmentalist' strategies that combined economic growth, state power and redistribution to the constituencies of key movements. At the same time, popular movements were often so disappointed by the results of independent states in the hands of urban elites, local landowners and international business interests that a third wave of movements took place in and against these states within what in Asia and Africa was a very few years of independence – considerably more, of course, in Latin America where some of the most radical struggles took place. In some places, peasant struggles and working-class unrest had never gone away, and burst to the surface in one country after another, with outcomes ranging from the Indonesian state's massacre of perhaps a million communists in 1965 and Mexico's massacre of students in 1968 to the Maoist-linked peasant struggles of the Indian 1960s and 1970s, as well as conflicts over national boundaries such as the Biafran war in Nigeria. The new states' power was increasingly contested.

THE MOVEMENTS OF 1968

Parallel to this attempt at radicalising independence, 1968 in the global North saw a decisive challenge to welfare state and state socialist attempts at compromise with popular movements. Whether in Prague, in Paris or in Derry, or in the 'long 1968' (from the mid-1950s to the mid-1970s) that includes the US Civil Rights Movement and East European dissidence, feminism and the struggle against nuclear power, popular movements challenged the state and the social order *both* in the name of those excluded from the formal interest compromise – women, ethnic and racial minorities, new and peripheral working-class categories, countercultural groups etc. – *and* in the name of a challenge to top-down power, whether technocratic, redistributive or founded on ethnic domination.

In Czechoslovakia, reformists sought 'socialism with a human face', in opposition to Soviet-dominated state socialism and the police state. In France, what was then the largest general strike in human history went hand in hand with students taking over the universities. In Northern Ireland, the sectarian power of Ulster Protestants was challenged by disadvantaged Catholics. Around the world, the logic of empire, war and Cold War was challenged, not least in opposition to the war in Vietnam pursued by the US and supported by its allies. More generally, these movements levelled a powerful critique at the mass-media 'spectacle' and the consumption-based ideal offered as a form of social pacification. They questioned the instrumental logic which saw work, science and rationality as defining of human existence.

What characterised 1968 above all else was the dramatic assertion of popular self-organisation: workers occupying factories, students occupying universities and running their own courses, actors or media staff running their own theatres or radios, communities taking over the streets of their own cities. Everywhere, it seemed, people were putting democracy into practice in their own lives. This radically reshuffled the cards of popular politics, replacing faith in top-down political parties and charismatic leaders as the normal mode of left organisation with a broad commitment to genuinely collective organisation at the grassroots, seeking democracy within movement organisations and not simply as something to be aimed for in a future state.

Nowhere did the movements of 1968 succeed in their own terms; but everywhere the impact of 1968 left the legitimacy of top-down state decision-making fatally undermined. In the west, a conservative gender and sexual order came under long and sustained attack and new generations of migrants struggled to assert themselves against official and popular racism. Technocracy was challenged around nuclear power plants and environmental destruction, by urban squatting and radical countercultures, by radical movements within education, health and mental health. The logic of Cold War was repeatedly challenged by movements against nuclear weapons, the war in Vietnam and future foreign adventures. In the east, 1968 and subsequent dissident movements raised many of the same issues in their own, difficult environments; the hostile official response helped lead towards the slow death of belief in state socialism even in those countries where it had been popular at the end of the war.

As Hilary Wainwright has noted, the impact of these movements was then used from above, in the face of the failure of welfare state and state socialist compromises, to clear the ground for the rise of neoliberalism as a strategy for capitalist development that would seek to limit redistribution by disaggregating collective action and converting what had once been social movement demands into questions of individual choice and opportunity, from commodified subcultures to women in the boardroom. The popular movements of 1989–1990 that overthrew state socialism in Eastern Europe, brought about the break-up of the Soviet Union and challenged Chinese state power head-on in Beijing and elsewhere would inherit these contradictions.

MODERNITY AND SOCIAL MOVEMENTS

I will discuss more recent waves of movements below, but even this very brief sketch shows just how central popular movements have been in the making of the modern world. Remove this perspective and you have 'a tale . . . full of sound and fury, signifying nothing', with no sensible way to explain the constant making and remaking of 'countries' (states and societies), their differences from one another and their interrelations. Most people on the planet live, today, in states that have been fundamentally remade by social movements within living memory. Miss this point, and we will understand little else.

Each of these waves of social movements and revolution, whatever the ultimate outcome, represents a real moment of weakness for the 'hegemonic' power of the ruling class in one or more regions of the capitalist world-system: its ability to maintain itself in power through securing the consent of some social groups and effectively coercing others. Thus each wave also represents a significant change in the self-making and remaking of *popular* power in those parts of the world: even conservative outcomes normally entail a new way of incorporating popular agency, within the medium term if not immediately, because what the crisis has signified is their inability to continue as if that agency had not changed.

This does not mean that the outcomes are necessarily good ones. What defines these moments of crisis is that the new forces are often not sure how to proceed but feel they have to take the risk of doing so. Conversely, the ruling forces are often pushed into responding at the point they realise that there is a crisis, but before it is clear that they no longer have a chance of success. Hence, things can go either way – and often go in different directions in different places. Waves like that of 1848, which was essentially defeated everywhere within a short time, or 1989, which was in a sense successful everywhere bar China, are the exception rather than the rule. However, as the example of 1848 (or indeed 1968) shows, the broader crisis often has to be resolved by taking at least *some* popular demands on board: things do not continue as before.

Conversely, what seems like 'success' at the time is often very ambiguous; not everyone involved gets the world they hoped for. It was at one time reasonable to expect that universal suffrage, national independence, welfare states or an opening to cultural diversity would mean a complete social transformation; as we have repeatedly seen, however, they do not automatically mean an end to capitalism, the state, patriarchy or racial and ethnic hierarchies. In fact, what emerges is often a new formation in which some popular demands come to the fore and strike a deal with capitalism at the expense of others.

A particularly dramatic case of this, albeit not part of a wave in the sense discussed above, is the end of apartheid in South Africa, where the insurgent African National Congress (ANC) literally met with the International Monetary Fund (IMF) and agreed that the end of whites-only rule and the move to universal suffrage would not mean the nationalisation of the strategically central mining industries or a break with neoliberal capitalism. South Africa today sees a combination of ongoing electoral support for the ANC's role in ending apartheid, with its loss of several key cities, an increasing part of the trade union movement breaking with its traditional loyalty to the party (symbolised by the state killing of independently organised miners in 2012), a much wider groundswell of community-based struggles over services and against neoliberalism and most recently a new wave of student struggles. Most of those involved understand their battle as a development and fulfilment of the real promise of the liberation struggle, a radicalisation rather than any kind of attempt at return to apartheid; and this is characteristic of such moments.

This kind of irony was already familiar to the socialist, artist (and inventor of fantasy literature) William Morris in 1886, when one of his time-travelling characters reflected, '[People] fight and lose the battle, and the thing that they fought for comes about in spite of their defeat, and when it comes turns out not to be what they meant, and other [people] have to fight for what they meant under another name'. Popular struggles, and their effects, are not linear; but their effects are nonetheless real, and we live in the world they have shaped.

HAVING TO TAKE ORDINARY PEOPLE ON BOARD

In the longer term, this sequence shows a continually greater need to take popular power on board and to find new ways of seeking consent. The traditionalist right wing, in the French revolution and after, sought simple restoration: to return the peasantry, ordinary city-dwellers, slaves and colonists to a situation of political insignificance, where their role was simply to obey both their immediate feudal or imperial overlords in a chain going up to the divine right of kings and the highest religious authorities, in return for their overlords making traditional paternalistic concessions. Restorationist fantasies always overestimated what was possible: popular bread riots and agrarian secret societies, the self-assertion of the local gentry and merchant groups, religious radicalism and slave revolts, to say nothing of native resistance in the Americas, had been recurring features of what reactionaries, those who wanted to turn back the clock to before 1789, imagined as a purely top-down form of power.

One effect of these fantasies is that it was impossible to recognise that peasants and *sans-culottes* might have had perfectly good reasons for rebelling, or even have been capable of doing so independently. The revolution must therefore have been caused by a secret elite – of philosophers, of Freemasons, of Jews, of Illuminati. Such conspiracy theories remain a staple of right-wing thought today, as an alternative to recognising that ordinary people may be able both to notice when they are exploited and oppressed and to do something about it.

In the century and a half that followed the French Revolution, the programme of a return to the *ancien régime* became less and less credible as a strategy for power. Its last major hurrah in Europe, the restoration after 1848, was followed over the following two decades by one parliamentary concession after another in different countries. These were not democratic in any contemporary sense, but gave the middle classes some say in what became increasingly parliamentary monarchies, and restructured dynastic states, inherited by particular ruling houses, towards nation-states founded on a sense of 'the people' as defined by nation, language and culture, a claim which was more radical in some contexts and more conservative in others.

This new state model would become absolutely dominant in Europe after the collapse of empires in 1918–1919.

Yet between the Paris Commune of 1871 and the continent-wide upheavals between 1916 and 1923, it became clear that this too was not enough and that the urban working classes and peasantry had definitively become political actors who could not be put back in their box and excluded from politics. This process was resisted: on left and right, the expectation was that formal political equality would mean large-scale redistribution and an egalitarian society. As we now know, the outcomes were far from this; and yet the pressure for democratic states to engage in *some* form of redistribution has been constant and powerful, in particular up to the 1970s. Even today, the scale of redistribution in Europe is far above where it was in 1918. Saying this is no defence of the present order: it is to recognise how far it has to take our needs on board even in a period of neoliberal austerity, and the limits beyond which it cannot risk pushing people, limits which in most cases we have not yet arrived at in a Europe where ruling classes still have some inherited sense of this practical reality and the potential strength of popular movements.

In the mid-twentieth century, the long history of urban working-class people self-organising to meet their own needs – through friendly societies and other collective responses to sickness or accidents, old age or unemployment; funeral clubs and funds to support widows and orphans; credit unions; food and land schemes; schools and adult educational projects; and above all trade unions – was in various ways incorporated into the political order. At times, as in Norway, this came about through alliances with the peasant movement after a period of intense strikes; at others, as in Germany, conservative elites introduced social insurance to try to defang a rising socialist movement. In Britain, the National Health Service came about as a response to popular pressures following the Depression and World War II, and so on. The multiple 'worlds of welfare capitalism' (and the varied arrangements of state-socialist and national-developmentalist states) nonetheless all represented an attempt by states of different political hues to handle these powerful demands from below.

RIGHT-WING POPULISM

Thus, popular classes became constant actors on the European political scene. In this context, what had originally been described as Bonapartism – rallying 'the people' behind a charismatic national leader – became an important early model for how to square the circle between the growing political agency of the large majority of people (well before universal suffrage; the vote was limited by wealth in most countries until after World War I and by gender until even later) and the defence of capitalist and aristocratic wealth and power. As a young Sicilian aristocrat responded to the liberal-nationalist unification of Italy in Lampedusa's novel *The Leopard*, 'If we want everything to stay as it is, everything has to change'.

Of course, not everything did remain the same: to maintain the essence of class power, many concessions, not least economic and political ones, had to be made. Welfare states, in this sense, are not simply a veneer over capitalist reality; it is in no sense a denial of the fundamental capitalist situation to say that they did meet many needs of the core organised groups (while excluding many others). Indeed, there remains a strong constituency in the global North, albeit largely unrepresented by contemporary political parties, of people who would happily return to the welfare arrangements of the 'thirty glorious years' after the war.

Bonapartism, and its later nineteenth-century variants such as Boulangisme in France and the Primrose League in England, had found themselves faced towards the end of the century by a far more strongly organised working class – structured in increasingly effective union federations and socialist parties, with their own press and public meetings, structures of economic solidarity discussed above, women's and youth organisations, sports and leisure groups, cultural and educational institutions – and eventually followed suit. Fascism, as a response, involved not only the call of the nation and the leader, but also plebiscites to demonstrate popular support, mass involvement in party organisations of all kinds (not just party membership but again labour, farming, women's and youth groups) and limited kinds of visible redistribution in the form of roads and rearmament programmes, workers' holidays and so on. Finally, in the postwar period, the Catholic Church – which had been formally opposed to democracy since Italian unification had taken over the Papal States – made its peace and supported the formation of Christian Democratic parties, enabling mass political organisation on an explicitly religious basis. Ireland, like many other postcolonial societies, had combined both elements in the mass religious organisation and popular support for (electoral) nationalism that characterised the country from independence in the 1920s up to the 1960s.

Thus (outside of the late fascist regimes in Iberia and Greece), even the most viciously right-wing governments could not simply reduce ordinary people to political zeroes or totally ignore their economic demands. There was a constant pressure from below, a secular growth in popular movement potential which any regime that wanted to stay in power had to take into account in some way, *especially* if the goal was to minimise formal democracy and social equality. This is a crucial part of understanding collective agency: much of what I have described in the previous paragraph (and which can be called 'social movements from above') consists of the attempt to form collective political subjects which are intimately structured through their alliance with economic and state power and cultural hierarchy (religious power, racism, patriarchal sexual relations and so on) so that a substantial proportion of popular collective agency flows in a useful direction for elites.

POPULAR STRUGGLES BEYOND THE WEST

The previous section tells a particular west European story; while a US reader might feel that the emphasis on popular struggles and welfare states is too positive here, its most direct counterparts are state socialist, first in the Soviet Union and then, after World War II, in East and Central Europe, in China and elsewhere in the majority world. Just as Western Europe and North America are significant variants of a common history, so too there were huge differences between state socialisms. Nonetheless, it is important to note that they were in some cases formed by actual revolution or (as in Czechoslovakia, Laos or Cuba) with the incorporation of revolutionary movements into a wider geopolitical situation not of their own choosing. They also involved extensive popular organisation in many different structures as well as significant redistribution. At the same time, the pressure in most of these societies for economic development meant that in practice a state managerial class and the drive for industrialisation (or, in Central Europe, competitive industrial development) still acted in exploitative ways, although the gulfs in wealth were far less than in the west.

In the rest of the global South, Asian and African anti-colonial resistance had by the interwar period become the project of an educated urban elite eager to assert itself as the future leadership of a national state (which would often be imposed on a multi-ethnic reality, with tensions both pre-existing and encouraged by imperial rule). This nationalist elite needed at least the passive support of the peasants who formed the mass of these populations and of the strategically central urban workers (indigenous populations were typically left out of this equation), whether their organisation took the form of peasant movements, labour unions and socialist parties or more religious and ethnically based shapes.

Many different kinds of 'movement-become-state' developed out of this experience, with China and India representing different models and producing very different results in terms of popular involvement in and consent for power and the scale and nature of redistribution and welfare provision. Nonetheless, it is broadly possible to describe most postindependence societies (state socialist and otherwise) as national-developmentalist, with elite commitment to the project of economic development for the whole country enabling some degree of redistribution even in those countries where capitalism and landholding patterns remained intact, and widespread popular support for the parties of the independence period. Latin America's much earlier political independence, and the different paths of popular organisation in much of Asia as against Africa, again mark out strong variations within this picture.

ENTER NEOLIBERALISM

What, then, of the present? In the 'First World', a turn to neoliberalism and against welfare states took place from the 1970s on, symbolised by the electoral victories of Thatcher and Reagan and their defeats of the miners and air traffic controllers, respectively, followed by the partial dismantling and thorough-going restructuring of much of the welfare state. The Scandinavian path to neoliberalism, like continental Western Europe's, did not follow an identical route, and popular capacity for resistance (if rarely anything more) remained somewhat greater.

The state socialist 'Second World' largely collapsed under the pressure of mostly peaceful popular uprisings in 1989 and 1990. The aggressive neoliberalism that followed throve in the wasteland of collective action that followed the wholesale disappearance of previous forms of political engagement, with various forms of strongman politics and right-wing nationalism filling the void. In China, however, the People's Liberation Army found itself reconquering Beijing by force, an experience (like internal colonialism in Tibet and Xinjiang and its increasing sabre-rattling abroad) which has cast a long shadow on popular agency within 'socialism with Chinese characteristics'.

Meanwhile, the 'Third World' has been suffering IMF- and World Bank-led neoliberalisation since the 1970s, a process symbolised by the 1973 CIA-backed coup in Chile against the democratically elected Allende and the homicidal regime that followed, but affecting different countries and regions in different periods and in different ways. National-developmentalism as an economic strategy was abandoned; health, education, welfare and subsidies were cut to the bone; 'uncommercial' small farmers (those feeding themselves) were driven off the land; multinational companies were given free reign while unions were smashed.

Yet even in these contexts, most dictatorships proved impossible to sustain over time, despite the death squads and the torture chambers. With the old, statist left co-opted or cowed, the right-wing dictatorships 'transitioned' by the 1990s into what was often a merely simulated democracy. Neoliberal rules, whether written into structural adjustment packages, EU treaties or global trade agreements, massively constrained the areas where voting made any difference. This was made clearly visible in relation to the Greek crisis, where German finance minister Wolfgang Schäuble commented 'Elections change nothing. There are rules' and European Commission president Jean-Claude Juncker said 'There can be no democratic choice against the European treaties'.

This situation enables the continued undercutting of previous popular gains in terms of general redistribution, the provision of services and workplace power, as well as a new wave of 'accumulation by dispossession': the commodification of many things, from indigenous land to water provision, that were once owned on some more collective basis. Neoliberalism's survival to date, but also the roots of its current crisis, has something to do with the political credit accumulated by these previous social formations.

The popular vote in many countries still goes to social-democratic, Christian-democratic or independence-era parties once associated with the construction of welfare states or other forms of clientelist redistribution. This can remain true for long periods even after these parties have abandoned such politics in favour of hard-line neoliberalism. As the South African example shows, however, this form of accumulated political credit does not last for ever.

Yet, popular resistance (or its potential) in many countries means that there is still a long way to go before reaching ground zero in terms of the neoliberal rollback of redistribution, and its effects are felt unevenly across different social groups. Thus, we see a general trend globally towards greater coercion and political fragmentation, with a key feature being the attempt to break up forms of collective political agency that could bring these different groups and issues together and speak for popular needs more broadly.

CONNECTING ISSUES, SEPARATING PEOPLE

At first glance, the major waves of social movement and revolution discussed above might seem to have primarily revolved around issues of class and state, which can lead to the false conclusion that these are somehow 'master issues', against which others are secondary. Yet the single largest of all these waves – which created most present-day states – was organised around the issues of imperialism and colonialism, race and ethnicity, while tying these to the struggles of peasants seeking land and urban workers. Moreover, movements *from above* have almost always sought in various ways to base themselves on defence of the nation and of the family, whether they have couched these in primarily religious or primarily secular terms. Conservatives have consistently appealed not only to men, but also to women who identify themselves primarily with their ascribed role in different social orders.

Or put another way: it is true that while women have tended to seize opportunities to resist and escape from patriarchy, there has been a consistent strand of women's organising which has accepted religious, conservative and racist or nationalist identities and sought self-assertion within these. However, we can equally say that if the majority of the workers' movement has been broadly on the left, internationalist and supportive of women's rights there has been a consistent corporatist, nationalist/racist and sexually conservative strand.

Most fundamentally, we should not imagine *separate* women's, workers, nationalist or whatever movements which only concern themselves with these issues. Instead, we have different forms of political subject which are subject to constant tensions around these issues and which necessarily – implicitly if not overtly – represent one choice of direction as against another. Most broadly, movements from below can (indeed are forced to) choose between alliance with each other's struggles or the attempt to assert one's own interests *as structured within the given social order* and hence at the expense of one another. From above, the hope is to purchase consent (for nationalism or racism, for patriarchy, for capitalism) with concessions that do not threaten the social order: a good deal for elites, if it can be arranged.

It is unsurprising, then, that it is precisely in the periods *between* waves, when major change does not seem to be on the agenda and it is hard enough to mobilise people on one issue, that movements tend to be separated from one another and most likely to seek alliances with what they believe to be progressive elite fractions in order to pursue integration within the (usually national) social order. Or put another way: when popular organisations have been shredded (like unions) or co-opted (like centre-left parties), it is easier for would-be alternative elites (women in the boardroom, black celebrities, working-class racists) to seem like the only game in town. Conversely, one of the first signs that serious social change is on the cards is when the voices within individual movements that argue for alliances with other movements come to the fore, and the possibility of a wider transformation comes to feel like a real possibility.

Such periods also represent – as oral histories repeatedly underline – moments of personal transformation. After all, we are not *only* workers or welfare recipients, women or gay men, ethnic minorities or racially dominated: often, even usually, we are several of these together. Most people in the global North, for example, are employees and beneficiaries of different kinds of welfare, health and education provision. Women form a majority of almost all populations (and even more of adult populations given life expectancy), and LGBTQI (lesbian, gay, bisexual, trans, queer, intersex) numbers are not small. A high proportion of us are migrants, indigenous or minorities who do not form part of the dominant ethnic or racial group; some of us have disabilities or mental health issues; others choose to live more or less outside cultural norms – while all of us are threatened by climate change and ecological destruction. It is a moment of awakening to take this greater range of our own experience on board, to say nothing of listening to our families, friends, neighbours, colleagues and acquaintances about their experience – and to decide to do something about it.

JOINING THE DOTS

In 1995, the Nigerian activist Ken Saro-Wiwa sat in military detention awaiting execution. A member of the indigenous Ogoni people of the Niger Delta, he led the nonviolent resistance to Shell's gas and oil activities in Ogoni territory, which were poisoning the water, land and air that this small fishing and farming population depended on for survival. At one point in 1993, perhaps as many as 60 per cent of the entire Ogoni population took part in protests against Shell. The then military dictatorship, with close ties to the oil industry, responded brutally. Special forces destroyed village after village, killing perhaps one to two thousand people and making tens of thousands homeless, raping women and girls and torturing detainees; as I write, Amnesty International is calling for criminal prosecutions of Shell for its complicity in this violence.

Saro-Wiwa and eight other Ogoni leaders were imprisoned on trumped-up charges of murder, tried by a military court and condemned to death. Throughout this process, Saro-Wiwa was writing to an Irish solidarity activist, Sister Majella McCarron, letters which were smuggled out in the basket used to bring him bread in jail. Many years after his execution, I was lucky enough to see these letters, when Majella donated them to my university on foot of our students' long involvement with the campaign against Shell's activities in Erris, NW Ireland; two colleagues and I edited and published the letters as a record of Saro-Wiwa's activism.

When writing about the book to people who know nothing of Saro-Wiwa or Ogoni, though, it is hard to know how to tell the story. Was this an ecological struggle, or one against the oil industry in particular? Was it a human rights conflict, or a struggle for democracy? Is the theme one of economic inequality and ownership of natural resources? Is it a case of indigenous self-assertion against the central state, or for that matter the nonviolent tactics which Saro-Wiwa successfully argued for?

The answer, of course, is 'all of the above': these different issues and themes connect with one another in the reality of what is still a desperately poor, environmentally damaged, politically suppressed but well-organised population in struggle – and with the wider global issues that come together in opposition to the oil industry: poverty, climate change, corruption and power. The strength of the Ogoni struggle, however, lies in part in making these connections, and not simply trying to further one of these (most obviously, in practice, seeking better rewards for local political interests in return for tolerating Shell's continued activities). When we join the dots, we find ourselves asking much bigger questions – and working with the much wider groups of people who do not stand to benefit from any politically easy solution.

THE WORLD THAT MOVEMENTS MADE

More broadly, social movements have been central to achieving much of what we hope to take for granted today. Our common-sense awareness of just how important 'rights' are and how many forces would like to remove or undermine them reflects this fact. Social movements only exist through constantly enforcing the rights of political organisation (notably the freedom of speech and assembly) in practice, while freedom of expression and religion go back to earlier popular struggles against absolutism and religious power which are still ongoing in parts of the world today, not least Ireland. Everywhere, too, women's rights, along with the right to sexual freedom and LGBTQI demands, have to be constantly fought for, defended and extended in the teeth of substantial opposition of different kinds. So too with the right to cultural diversity – whether the right to speak one's own language or the right to live according to one's own lights: these have been the subject of many battles large and small, from the countercultural youth movements that provoked moral panics in east and west in the postwar decades to ongoing struggles over minority and regional culture in many countries.

I have a badge somewhere that reads 'Unions: the folks who brought you the weekend'. The weekend, along with the eight-hour day and (where we have it) the right to paid holidays and sick leave, as well as all sorts of protections against sickness and injury, unemployment and old age, were first fought for in the labour struggle or self-organised among the urban poor before states and employers were forced to the table, in some cases seeking to make concessions on their own terms rather than lose the kinds of battles they had watched in neighbouring countries. Free education and health provision too, to the extent they exist, are as much the product of social movement struggles as of the benevolence or managerial strategies of states: something that becomes clear each time our own state tries to cut one or another and we find out who is capable of effectively resisting the process.

Alongside movements 'internal' to capitalist society, we should pay close attention to the struggles of indigenous populations in resisting its expansion: in the Americas since the 1970s in particular, forming a fundamental part of resistance to the oil industry in Canada and the US, in the form of the long-lasting Zapatista rebellion in Mexico, or underpinning radical attempts to make different kinds of states in the Andes while resisting the 'neo-extractivism' which has meant greater destruction of indigenous livelihoods through mining, logging and so on in order to fund 'progressive' policies elsewhere.

In India, too, the enormous struggle against mega-dam projects on the Narmada River, peasant resistance to mining, drilling and logging or to land grabs for industrial megaprojects are regularly centred in indigenous populations, as is the long-running conflict between the state and Maoist guerrillas in eastern India. So too, for much resistance in a country like Indonesia – or to Shell in the Niger Delta. While following fundamentally different rhythms to other movements, recent decades have seen indigenous struggles become increasingly significant in many countries, setting 'limits to capital' of a different kind.

Almost all of the gains mentioned above, in most places, are unfinished battles, for a good reason: they were achieved in the teeth of other forces who bitterly opposed their introduction. Where they are currently taken for granted, this is because neither side sees a realistic opportunity of overturning the basic parameters of the present situation. For example, it is politically impossible in most countries with publicly funded education to resist the *principle* that it should be available to all up to a certain age, even though neoliberals are busy hollowing the principle out in practice. Similarly, while abortion is still a hotly contested issue, attempts at imposing Catholic teaching on contraception have been quietly dropped in most countries: as birth rates show, the vast majority of practising Catholics also practise birth control. However, in times of crisis like the recession of the late 1970s and early 1980s, or again after the crash of 2007/2008, we see determined attempts to break these rights: to create union-free workplaces, for example, or to impose bailout agreements that reduce basic social provision to meaningless levels in Greece; regular police violence against protestors and the surveillance of every aspect of activist organising; and so on.

THE 'MOVEMENT OF MOVEMENTS' AGAINST NEOLIBERALISM

I suggested above that the long 1968 is best seen as representing popular resistance to the top-down arrangements of western welfare states, eastern state socialisms and southern national-developmentalism. This resistance was led by social actors who were excluded from participation in central interest representation processes but also oppressed by the forms of state power, workplace control and imposed cultural homogeneity characteristic of the highpoint of these arrangements. In the 1970s, in particular, after the defeat of the first, 'revolutionary' moment of these struggles, it seemed that alliances between radical versions of these struggles with a global agenda were the wave of the future: the articulation of a different ('red-green', but also feminist and libertarian) vision of society around the massive opposition to nuclear power plants in the west, dissident visions of socialism with a human face, intellectual and political alliances such as socialist feminism, gay socialism, black feminism and so on.

In the 1980s, it would become clear that neoliberalism was more than capable of co-opting isolated elements of each of these movements – arguably it had to do so in order to shore up its own legitimacy. Thus (for example), female, gay or black professionals used radical rhetoric to advance their own interests at the expense of the large majority of people in each of these categories; ecological and countercultural movements became channelled into forms of 'lifestyle' consumption; or defeated, demobilised and individualised working-class populations were targeted by right-wing media and politicians as bases of support for their racist, militarist and misogynist policies. Only in the later 1990s did it become possible, in some contexts, to remake earlier, radical alliances around shared opposition to neoliberalism (a term which acquired popularity precisely for its usefulness in this context).

In the late 1980s and early 1990s, a wave of Latin American dictatorships was replaced by formally democratic arrangements with little real social change. In the years that followed, however, a 'pink tide' of progressive or left-wing governments came to power on the back of a wide range of social movement struggles, covering three-quarters of the Latin American population by the mid-2000s. These governments varied not only in how they related to popular movements but also how far they sought a break with the international financial institutions (IMF/World Bank, World Trade Organisation, etc.) and US geopolitical hegemony more broadly. This wave is now receding in some countries and under sustained attack in others.

Movements' capture of the state was always very limited in some contexts where centre-left governments took power (Brazil, Chile, Argentina); after a period of success the Right has been able to use existing structures to roll back these changes in various ways. In more radical situations, a closer link between popular movements and radical parties led to partially transformed states in Venezuela, Bolivia and Ecuador. These too have come under increasing pressure, in part because of the weaknesses of Chavez' strongman politics but more substantially because 'neo-extractivism', the reliance on intensified extraction of raw materials, has not changed their fundamental dependence on a global scale (Venezuela's oil is worth far less than it once was) and (in Bolivia and Ecuador) has pitted indigenous movements defending their land against state willingness to force through extraction and infrastructure projects. With all these limitations, the variety and creativity of these movements and experiments is a fundamental resource for radical movements globally.

In the US, global justice alliances of environmentalists, trade unionists and radicals came together in the 1999 Seattle protest that defeated the World Trade Organisation but were effectively broken by the nationalist rallying cry of the 'war on terror' from 2001, returning in limited form in the later 2000s and in greater force in indigenous resistance to pipelines, Black Lives Matter and the many forms of resistance to Trump. In Western Europe, the earlier wave of struggle up to the police killing of Carlo Giuliani at the Genoa protest in 2001 fed into an enormous antiwar movement in 2003 and then into anti-austerity struggles as different as Iceland's saucepan revolution, the Spanish and Greek indignad@s of 2011, the more statist Portuguese left or Nuit Debout in France. In the Arab world, the wave of popular uprisings that threatened or toppled tyrants in 2011 also drew on earlier opposition to the 'war on terror' and ongoing tensions around Palestine. The decentralised and feminist revolution in Rojava (Syrian Kurdistan) is still developing despite the Turkish invasion.

Elsewhere, there are huge popular struggles both in Chinese industry and in the countryside, along with bitter resistance from indigenous and other movements in much of India, in both cases struggling to articulate themselves nationally let alone make powerful international connections. In other countries, the struggles in countries like Turkey from Gezi Park on, in South Africa for many years or more recently in Brazil are very much linked to a wider global 'movement of movements', even when they do not use this term. The implication here is that we should not so much think of a single, identical movement happening in many different places as of many different movements, learning to work together in different ways, around a shared opposition to neoliberalism but without losing any of their own diversity.

Indeed, there is an extent to which movement-to-movement networking globally has displaced the Internationals of political parties and trade unions which defined the mid-twentieth century left. Even if international audiences find issues easier to understand when framed in terms of states and policies, they do so primarily as social movement participants rather than (as in previous decades) members of left parties. To take one example, the membership of the Democratic Socialists of America, often presented as the radical hope for the US left, is currently estimated at a mere eighteen thousand people. More positively, what the 'movement of movements' has meant is a constant and necessary attention to the complex reality of different struggles in different places, a grounding of the attempt to develop a wider challenge to neoliberalism in the lived reality of people's concrete lives. This also means refusing the ways in which neoliberalism, and the global domination of

Anglophone media, encourage a flattening homogenisation of this real speci-
ficity into a single, simplifying, image.

ELITES LOOK FOR A WAY FORWARD

What Alf Nilsen and I have called the twilight of neoliberalism was heralded
by the anti-capitalist and alterglobalist 'movement of movements' that has
challenged neoliberal legitimacy in many ways since around the turn of the
millennium and with renewed vigour since the economic crash of 2007–2008.
There is now a constant search for new political forms that could stabilise
the situation. We are seeing a shift towards nationalist authoritarianism in
states as different as India and Turkey (where Modi and Erdoğan have some
mass basis in right-wing religious parties and their associated organisations),
Russia (where Putin's power has strong Bonapartist tendencies given the
enormous difficulty of popular organisation across the huge differences in
society) or Egypt (where the religious-conservative takeover of the 2011 revolution by the Muslim Brotherhood has given way to a reassertion of military
dictatorship with Western support). The politics of Law and Justice in Poland
or Viktor Órban in Hungary, or those of Trump in the US and Brexit in Britain, represent other variants again on this general pattern, all responding to
the crisis of consent of an older neoliberalism with the apparently obvious
answer of racist and nationalist authoritarianism.

How successful any of these experiments will be in the medium term is
another question, and one which needs answering very differently in different countries. What can be confidently stated is that a crucial question in
each context is the *organisation of popular consent*, in other words social
movements, from above and below. Simply voting for Trump or Brexit, for
example, does not add up to any kind of more active mobilisation, and struggles to find a sustainable organisational form; right-wing trolling does not
quite fill the void. In the US, resistance to the right has been a fertile source
of organisational innovation, while in Britain Momentum in the Labour Party
is proving surprisingly successful at mobilising. In both countries, however,
progressive forces have an uphill battle because of the previous third of a century's destruction or institutional co-optation of the historical organisations
of popular power and activism. The tendency to interpret issues in purely
parliamentary terms is one effect of this history.

What all of this means, of course, as in any crisis, is that *collective agency
matters*. Who will win in the crisis cannot be discovered by reading the
tea leaves of political economy, or by peering into the abyss that is right-
wing politics and seeing what its worst exponents *hope* for. It can only be
discovered collectively and in practice, in our attempts to resist and build

alternatives – and their success or failure at including different social groups, building alliances and constructing a credible vision that ordinary people feel happy to get involved with. Alongside the upsurge of activism in the US, we could mention popular mobilisation around climate justice, the outpouring of hospitality and solidarity in response to the Syrian refugee crisis, the solidarity with Greece in the summer of 2015 or global feminist organising around sexual harassment. None of these have as yet found stable and sustainable organisational forms, but in different ways they all show that there is a 'real potential', in the sense outlined in chapter 4, for something different, 'from below and on the left' as the Zapatistas say, to emerge as a political actor pointing the way towards a better future.

THINKING TODAY'S MOVEMENTS SERIOUSLY

It is important, in all of this, to avoid the kind of criticism which assumes that mentioning social movements is to claim that they have already won – and that pointing out their limitations or defeats is a sufficient dismissal. Popular movements, in most times and places, face opponents who are far more powerful, wealthier and culturally dominant. Their own successes are rarely as simple as electoral ones; and, as we can see with the Greek referendum of 2015, such victories do not always mean what we think. *Because* movements' opponents have not gone away, and neoliberalism remains in power – even if, as I argue, holed below the waterline in terms of its popular legitimacy – we are talking about a dramatic conflict between actors, not some sort of cultural transformation in which a single organisation or event can change everything. That is not how empires, religious power, older forms of capitalism or patriarchy have come to an end; and it is historically illiterate to expect social change in the present to be any less complex and contested, or any more transparent to its participants than in the past.

Instead, I want to tell a different sort of story. Following the largely defensive 'IMF riots' of the 1980s, the Zapatista revolution in southeast Mexico inspired a new wave of radical alliance formation around outright opposition to neoliberalism and a refusal to participate within existing structures shaped around it. The Peoples' Global Action network gave birth to a series of dramatic summit protests around the world in which 'we met one another in the streets'. This was perhaps the clearest single organisational genealogy within a much wider coming-together of movements that underpinned popular uprisings in South America, from the Bolivian water war to the Argentinian revolutionary moment of 2001; antiwar resistance in the North connecting with a new wave of popular struggle in the Arab world; Northern indignad@s and Occupy movements, bringing together mass popular participation in the attempt to create real democracy and resist neoliberalism; the 'Arab Spring' of 2011, where in a country like Egypt workers, students, nationalists, the Muslim Brotherhood, football fans, defecting elements of the state and middle-class liberals came together; and more isolated struggles elsewhere, from South Africa to Indonesia.

In Seattle, computer activists outraged by mainstream media misrepresentation of protests created Indymedia as a tool for what would now be called citizen journalism, directly reporting on the events from many different sources. Remaining live after the protest, Indymedia multiplied worldwide and became a horizontal space for 'peer-to-peer' discussion, which not only foreshadowed today's Web 2.0, with its social media and commenting back on articles, but also in many cases fed into it both personally and technically. In Brazil, an alliance of Latin American and west European activists and intellectuals created the World Social Forum as a critical mirror to the elite World Economic Forum at Davos. The social forum movement, bringing together movements in a space of discussion rather than action, also went worldwide, with continental, national and sometimes city-based social forum events or ongoing movements.

All of this enabled the development and articulation of shared modes of organising and acting, which expressed existing tendencies in the remaking of popular culture in the twenty-first century but also earlier traditions of social movement practice which had survived underground (literally in some cases) and the articulation of the best practice among activists in the new, emerging movements. This is a very complex process, and it is important to avoid the simple celebration of newness, the flattening effects of journalistic clichés and lofty dismissals by those nostalgic for earlier modes of organising. What constitutes a 'movement of movements' in this context, though, is *both* the existence of many parallel histories or traditions *and* the many and varied kinds of connection they seek to build with one another, across great differences.

In different social groups and different continents, movement processes work very differently, as researchers regularly show. Indeed, part of what has happened in the antiwar movement, in Latin American struggles over the state, in European anti-austerity movements or the uprisings of 2011, is that different actors have sought to pull the process in different directions; and any attempt to homogenise the situation misses this basic fact. Movements grow out of specific, complex situations and respond to these in thoughtful, internally contested ways: they cannot be easily and simply equated to one another. Instead, what we see is the slow and difficult process of collective learning across time, conversations including new popular actors as they make themselves in struggle, tension between different strategies and approaches: not a simple 'onwards and upwards' but a difficult practical challenge of learning, communication and collaboration across great distances.

THE POLITICS OF SOCIAL MOVEMENTS RESEARCH

The account I have given thus far draws not only on academic research but also on what Gramsci called 'good sense', the struggle to make sense of our own experience and history from below. Good sense, for Gramsci, clashes with 'common sense', the clichés repeated in school and the media, in the pub and in family gatherings – ways of shaping our understanding, or expressing our discontent with the world, that do not challenge the existing order. Articulating more fully and openly what we do know, and thinking it through together, are crucial parts of the process of disaggregating popular consent for the way things are, and bringing about another kind of world.

Part of that process, in fact a central part, is 'learning from each other's struggles': coming to have a better sense of the experience of different social groups, in other parts of the world, and for that matter our longer histories, so that we do not simply wind up with a more radicalised version of our personal starting point but with a broader sense of 'we', one more adequate to the struggles we face, the alliances we need to make, the opponents we have to overcome and the wider world we are operating within.

Where, in all of this, is research on social movements and revolutions? In my own work, I have been strongly critical of 'actually existing' social movement studies, and this book does not follow the freakonomists and evolutionary psychologists in proposing ourselves as some new master science. Unlike economics, which now exists as a kind of orthodox theology for neoliberalism, with high status among policymakers and very little space for intellectual diversity, or pseudoscientific cults which really operate as the intellectual wing of racism and sexism, social movements research is such a varied field that it can hardly play this role, even if it wanted to.

There are certainly some more tightly defined approaches within it, such as the US-based orthodoxy which has its own canon within which one must operate in order to be published in its own spaces. Thankfully, social movements are so widespread that reflection and commentary on them can hardly be contained within such a small space. Within history, a long-standing tradition of Marxist and other social historians, along with subaltern studies research in Asia, contemporary feminists and oral historians, has explored some of the world's most dramatic popular struggles. Exploration of 'resistance', in the sense used by Foucault or the very different North American sense of non-violence as an almost codified form of action, has its own spaces which coexist with anarchist and Marxist studies of everyday workplace and peasant conflict at a very low level.

The study of revolutions (often divorced from that of social movements) is split between American universities, where it has historical roots in Cold War foreign policy aimed at defeating them; traditions in the global South where what is at stake is the history of one's own state formation; the European study of our ambiguous revolutionary experiences; and anarchist and Marxist analysis of how different revolutions failed or succeeded. Within feminism, Black Studies, LGBTQI research, indigenous studies, urban studies and even parts of natural science, attention to popular movements relevant to these issues fluctuates across time, discipline and countries. There is also a long-standing tradition in cultural studies (which came out of an attention to informal and symbolic modes of popular resistance), the academic study of religion, literary studies, political philosophy and many other fields of thinking one's own subject of research through social movements and collective agency in different forms. Elsewhere, too, it is hard to think seriously about educational theory, industrial relations, civil society, solidarity economy or welfare policy without discussing popular movements.

Social movements research, then, at its broadest is a conversation crossing many different ways of reflecting on how human beings struggle together, and it is all the richer for this. In fact one of its major contributions is precisely when it can show these interlinkages and connect up (for example) a subculture, an innovation in education, a particular kind of policy, popular memory of a revolution, a literary movement or everyday peasant culture with some experience or experiences of social movement. In this way, social movements research helps us to deepen our understanding of the world as it already is and to transform that understanding through seeing it as the products of our own collective agency – or as capable of being challenged and transformed collectively today where earlier struggles had failed.

Good research in the field resists the journalistic clichés that try to squeeze collective action into the sort of story that journalists know how to research – one organised around key individuals, style moments, formal politics or an influential book. Instead, researchers spend long periods of time in the field (or, for historical movements, reading their leaflets, magazines, posters, internal discussions and autobiographical accounts), getting a real feel for *how it works* when people come together, *outside* the everyday routines that mainstream media is comfortable with, to create a kind of thing they have sometimes never experienced before, against opponents with more power, resources and status and whose responses are uncertain.

Such research does not wind up, usually, producing the kind of 'movements good/movements bad' opinion beloved of social media, instant journalism and a certain kind of left. It certainly *draws attention to* movements that in the nature of things are rarely noticed unless they are in our immediate context (or suit our own countries when they challenge competing ones); but rather than presenting them as a unified whole, it shows the tensions, conflicts and learning processes involved as different interests and strategies are articulated and the conflict intensifies and changes. For activists, good work of this kind can help them better understand what it is they are doing. After all, learning in this kind of situation is won at a great human cost; the more we can learn from each other's struggles, the better for all of us.

This sort of research is really important when we are conscious of a problem in our own worlds but do not know how to solve it. Seeing what other movements have done is often a crucial first step in thinking what we could do and what might work. In a world where 'bad movements' or 'movement failures' are often held over our heads to dissuade us from taking action, it is really important to have a clear and realistic sense of how movements *actually* work, and not only what their opponents would like us to believe of them.

An important tradition within Marxist, anarchist, feminist and postcolonial studies is geared towards understanding not simply the learning processes within individual movements, but also something of how movement traditions develop and persist across time, transmitting some sense of learning and collective identity from one generation to the next (or, through migration and solidarity, from one place to the next); at the broadest sense, this raises the question of 'the making of the working class', or of 'the feminist movement', or of black political agency, or of indigenous resurgence, as one of how whole groups of people become not only collective subjects but also actors on the world stage over decades or centuries.

MOVEMENT THEORISING

These traditions themselves, and much of social movements research more generally, draw on movements' own processes of research and theorising. Different movements have different kinds of capacity and priority in this area, and it is usually challenging for movements to sustain independently over time. But many movement actors do understand the importance (for example) of highlighting movement struggles happening elsewhere and documenting our own as they are going on; of education and training which introduces participants to a wider understanding of movement struggles as well as practical techniques for workplace organising, nonviolent direct action or public mobilisation. Movements develop their own periodicals, films, summer camps, educational workshops or other structures to keep a wider understanding alive and prevent the movement from simply reacting to its opponents by enabling it to have a wider sense of possibility.

The academic versions of feminism and Marxism, indigenous and black studies, queer studies and community education all in different ways draw on these traditions. Some (Marxism most notably) have also sustained institutions of historical and political analysis and complex bodies of theoretical knowledge over many decades *outside* the academy, in the context of at times ferocious repression, vicious internal conflicts and against a background of huge poverty. In other traditions, theoretical work and practical research may depend on a handful of individuals, or may have largely been absorbed into the university.

But in the widest sense, social movements regularly return to the tasks of trying to learn from their own experience; trying to articulate those lessons theoretically in order to think about the big strategic picture; and trying to develop appropriate forms of education and training to return these ideas to the world of practice. We should be deeply grateful to them for doing so; without this process, neither the Civil Rights Movement nor trade unions, the women's movement nor the environmental movement would have had anything like the impact they have had on today's world. It may be clear by now why there is no 'book', written by an authoritative Expert, that can tell us what movements can be or what they should do: that book is written collectively, as movements try to *move* into a space which has never yet been occupied.

Chapter 3

Social Movements and the Left: Thinking 'the Social Movement in General'

In the Hamburg winter of 1990/1991, I spent long periods shivering in subzero temperatures outside the American consulate. Camped beside the frozen Alster lake, this was a peace vigil set up to protest the second Gulf War, which saw the US-led invasion of Iraq in response to Iraq's invasion of Kuwait, a classic 'war for oil' on both sides. We were part of a much broader peace movement in Germany, with large marches and some dramatic direct action by schoolchildren, large numbers of whom walked in circles around major street intersections and brought the city to a halt.

Initially, I had come to the camp as a liaison from the Hamburg Green-Alternative List, a radical movement-oriented part of the Green Party. As I stayed there, the party infighting brought on by German reunification and a series of difficult elections came to seem much less relevant than the ongoing vigil trying to avert mass loss of life. Parties did become relevant from another, and surprising, direction, though: the orthodox Communist Party (DKP) turned out to have large quantities of camping equipment that made it possible for us to keep the camp going through a hard winter.

It later transpired that the DKP, loyal to East Germany in the Cold War context, had maintained a small quasi-military group, training across the border until it fell in 1989. This would have been entirely irrelevant in an actual war but had presumably helped keep some party members active and feeling that they were doing something 'real'. We were in any case grateful for the tents, camp beds and heating gear, which were put to a less macho use.

From the Green Party to a peace camp to a communist private army, the relationships between social movements and other kinds of politics are not always as straightforward as one might imagine.

'THE LEFT' VERSUS 'SOCIAL MOVEMENTS':
A FALSE OPPOSITION

Chapter 2 showed what an important part social movements play in shaping our history. We saw social change, state structures, political ideas and popular culture underpinned by struggles from below around class, race and nation, gender and sexuality and much more. You might think, then, that where you find radical ideas and debates, progressive organisations and parties, you would also find a lot of discussion of social movements: after all, if these popular struggles matter, don't people who care about them move towards the left? Sometimes, and in some places, this is true; but often much of what calls itself 'the left' today has little or nothing to say about social movements. This chapter is particularly written for people who are interested in politics, but think of that mostly in terms of parties, states and policies, and see movements as irrelevant. It asks why there might at times be a gulf between 'the left' and 'social movements', how we can think about what 'the left' is from the perspective of movements, and what kinds of relationship might be possible between the two.

For many people on the English-speaking left, the phrase 'social movements' has come to carry a lot of baggage. Often, it is understood as specifically referring to 'new social movements', a series of struggles which returned to prominence (most were not new issues) in the radical wave of the 1960s and 1970s, including the US Civil Rights Movement and other anti-racist movements, women's liberation, gay and lesbian struggles, the ecology and anti-nuclear power movements, struggles against war and nuclear weapons and so on. In this understanding, the phrase 'social movements' is read as part of very specific arguments within the British and US left about the role of culture and identity, the changing shape of the economy and the working class, and social movements are often understood as something which is by definition opposed to political parties and trade unions.

But this particular definition is rather odd. After all, Marxism in particular – often understood in this particular way of thinking as the opposite of 'social movements' – comes out of what has been variously called the workers' movement or the labour movement. In fact, the original point of the phrase 'new social movements', in the continental New Left of those decades, was to ask what the relationship of this new wave of movements was to older social movements – meaning not only the labour movement but also nationalism, peasant struggles, religious movements, movements of the far right, democratic movements and so on.

These older movements regularly had (and sometimes still have) political parties, at times unions, their own journals, intellectuals and many of the things which are now identified with how 'the left' organises and social movements are supposed not to. Furthermore, as Colin Barker has shown, Marx's own work contains a much broader conception of social movement in which not only labour conflicts but also radical-democratic politics, the Irish or Polish national struggles, battles over land or forest rights, opposition to imperialist wars, women's emancipation and the struggle against established religion all played a part. We need to step back from a clumsy vocabulary which positions 'the left' and 'social movements' as two different things, and restart the clock on our own thinking.

Talking to comrades and companer@s, it is often clear that they assume that the main reason for writing about a particular form of struggle is to celebrate it, and to propose it as The Way Forward. In this view, there is a constant battle between (for example) talk about parties and talk about movements. The assumption is that we should only write about ideal examples of whichever we believe in, in order to propose that mode of organisation, often for other countries and situations. In this picture, there is no real difference in (say) the issues at stake in organising in Ireland (where a massive working-class movement has just defeated the state on the commodification of water) or England, in the US (with its remarkable wave of mobilisations from Black Lives Matter on) or Germany, in Greece or Argentina (depending on our preferences) and in France or Canada. The real role of 'the left' or movement researchers would then be to act as international cheerleaders for the best model, be that Chavez or the Zapatistas, Syriza or Rojava, Argentinian piqueteros or South African shanty-town dwellers – in the belief that whatever model represents 'international best practice' will work just as well in one place as in another.

BEYOND CELEBRATION AND CONDEMNATION

The best Marxist traditions of thinking about social movements, however – those of the 'British Marxist historians' like E. P. Thompson and Christopher Hill, for example – do not take this approach. Their starting point was the movements that actually existed in particular times and places, with all their limitations. As Thompson wrote,

> I am seeking to rescue the poor stockinger, the Luddite cropper, the 'obsolete' hand-loom weaver, the 'utopian' artisan, and even the deluded follower of Joanna Southcott, from the enormous condescension of posterity. Their crafts and traditions may have been dying. Their hostility to the new industrialism may have been backward-looking. Their communitarian ideals may have been fantasies. Their insurrectionary conspiracies may have been foolhardy. But they lived through these times of acute social disturbance, and we did not.

This is no less true today when we are commenting on an online newspaper article in English about struggles in a shanty town on the far side of the world. Of course, one thing these historians – and in more recent generations writers like Sheila Rowbotham, Peter Linebaugh or Marcus Rediker – were fully aware of was that the movements they researched *lost*.

At times they lost because of practical political mistakes they made: in England, for example, things might have gone differently with the Levellers or the Chartists. More commonly, though, they lost because they were small movements facing impossible odds, meaning that the present-day left habit of 'drawing lessons from X' (in practice, suggesting that if only a given movement had had the right line they could have won) rarely makes sense – and the 'enormous condescension of posterity' is misplaced. However, movements like the Diggers or the Corresponding Societies were important even when they lost: they expressed the best of what the radical poor were able to articulate intellectually, organisationally and in terms of visions of the future, and they left important legacies in terms of political traditions.

With the study of present-day movements, too, in practice good researchers often write about the movements they know through their own activism, rather than parachuting into movements which they have decided from the outside to be worthy of their attention. Nor are most other participants sitting on the sidelines, waiting to decide what movements they should align themselves with, in the kind of strategic game that some critics seem to imagine. Most commonly, in fact, movements *respond* to something happening in their participants' lifeworlds, so that the idea that movement A is worthwhile and movement B isn't simply misses the (materialist) point.

Being inside movements as well as reflecting on them, the best of present-day research in the area (such as the activist researchers who write for the journal *Interface*) has no great interest in cheerleading or condemning. After all, it is hard to seriously imagine that celebrating working-class community activism in the pages of an international left publication would do more than attract a few revolutionary tourists, or that condemning the ideas of people occupying farmland to prevent an airport being built will convince them to leave and join an editorial committee instead. Like other activists, researchers often oscillate between moments of deep despair and moments of hope in relation to the movements they are involved in: unsurprisingly so, because people typically get involved in movements when success through 'normal channels' seems excluded but alternative forms of activism hold out the possibility of winning in unusual (hence unpredictable) ways.

The questions activist researchers ask are different ones, *more* political in that they are far more closely tied to the debates among present-day movement participants. Prominent among these are discussions on how to organise and what kinds of action to take; arguments about internal democracy and decision-making; the question of whether this or that organising practice makes it easier or harder for women, migrants, working-class people and so on to get involved; and conflicts over who to make alliances with and where to draw the boundaries of the movement. Our research thus feeds into the process of movement democracy, with all its many faults. It is neither an advertisement for the movement nor a warning against participation, but rather an exploration of *what happens* when people in a particular society get involved with processes of social struggle.

There is an element of cursing the weather in objecting to the fact that people mobilise for this and not for that, or that when they come together they do so in this way and not in that way. Railing against the practical reality of what people do in movements, for political activists, means actively seeking *not* to understand it and proposing that what has convinced us personally (or what seems to work in our own lifeworlds) is *more right* or more real than what has motivated everyone else. If we do the latter, not only do we not understand movements or become any wiser individually, we also make ourselves unable to build serious alliances. We cannot become any better at relating our own organisations to newly arising movement struggles if our first concern is to have an *opinion* on the movement, rather than to understand what we can learn about the shape of popular struggle today from taking the time to listen and examine the movement more closely.

TRADITIONS OF THE LEFT

The tradition of writing I have discussed above comes out of a particular history within the left. Thompson's generation had become involved in orthodox communist politics under the impact of fascism and above all the European Resistance, a high point of popular struggle which saw at its peak in 1943/1945 collaboration between communists, socialists, anarchists, radical democrats and Trotskyists in opposing fascism and then the arrival of super-power armies on both sides of what would become the Iron Curtain.

In the west, empire and Cold War would set sharp limits to what popular power could achieve. In the east, Soviet power turned ever more clearly against popular movements, culminating in the brutal repression of the 1956 Hungarian uprising. One result of these experiences was that this generation left the communist parties, attempted to organise through improvised New Left structures and then committed itself more to supporting popular movements of different kinds. For different activists on the New Left this meant antiwar movements, the new forms of working-class struggle, the revolts of 1968, the women's movement, the movement against nuclear power and so on. Dissident movements in Eastern Europe and the Soviet Union fought many of the same battles, challenging their own states and talking past the censors to unorthodox comrades abroad.

There are many other left histories in the world, and I do not want to place this particular history on a pedestal, except in one respect: it was a history of *acknowledging and learning* from the mistakes of past formations and attempting to draw practical conclusions. This commitment to learning was once a proud left tradition, but in the present context often the reverse is the case. To be on the left sometimes seems to mean a position of refusing to learn; even, today, celebrating a nostalgic 'communism' with no serious attempt to engage with the disaster that was Stalinism. At other times, it becomes a position of pure opinion, separate from actual popular struggle but elevated above it by a schoolmasterly wagging of fingers at the theoretical errors committed by ordinary people who are trying to resist the latest assault on their own lives.

If 'the Party' could once claim to be the memory of the class, now today it is all too often the amnesia of the class, an active celebration of refusing to learn from the mistakes of one's own tradition – since the real point is to act as apologists for that tradition. In this model, whatever theoretical and organisational points define a specific tradition have to be held up as correct in all times and all places, no matter what. Small wonder that such formations are rarely successful, because this is the politics of the stopped clock. Twice a day, any given time will of course be right. . .

A particularly unhelpful manifestation of this way of thinking is the two different sets of scales on which leftists sometimes weigh movements in commenting on contemporary struggles. For example, the argument might be that this or that movement (the 2011 'Occupy' protests in the US and UK, for example) was not just a failure in its own terms but that this failure was an inevitable result of some theoretical failure (horizontalism, for example) whose wrong-headedness is made visible precisely by the failure of Occupy. And yet this same criterion is not brought to bear on one's own party or group – which is almost certainly far smaller and with far less effect on the world. *We* (in our own particular tradition) are to be measured not in terms of how we are actually doing but in terms of (say) the historical significance of the Russian Revolution, or of what is 'objectively' needed in order to overcome capitalism today – never mind the fact that we are not within a million miles of being able to do so.

But what is sauce for the goose has to be sauce for the gander. If we want to allow our own organisations the luxury of being small, ineffective and crisis-ridden without concluding from this that we are making some fundamental theoretical mistakes, we have to give movements which are much larger and more effective and have managed to provoke some crisis in the existing order real credit for that. We can and should argue with them, but on fair and concrete terms that reflect the realities they are struggling with – rather than in terms of a wished-for future that is no closer for us than it is for the movements we criticise.

A HISTORICAL AND MATERIALIST ANALYSIS OF 'THE LEFT'

I want to propose a different, and more historically minded, analysis of the relationship between 'the left', parties and unions and popular struggle. We have seen just how painfully slow the struggle for democracy was. There were good reasons for this: popular movements and elites alike assumed (at the time entirely reasonably) that if the masses had equal political rights they would use them to redistribute wealth equally. In this context, as Thompson among others has shown, political rights – the freedom of speech and publication, the freedom to organise politically and to demonstrate, the freedom to join trade unions and form political parties, the rights of political refugees not to be deported to the states they were fleeing – were hotly contested and won with great difficulty and many limitations by various forms of liberal, radical-democratic, nationalist and labour struggles.

In this situation (in this respect closer to our own than we might like), popular movements struggled to maintain any kind of representation in the official public sphere. The First International (1864–1876), the first systematic attempt at international working-class organising, was killed as much by its association with the Paris Commune and subsequent repression as by the famous squabble between Marx and the anarchists. More commonly, until the very last decades of the nineteenth century and the start of the twentieth, working-class parties were unable to enter parliament (where there were meaningful parliaments to enter) so that the interests of working men and women developed peculiar and not always transparent relationships with individual politicians and journalists who represented the radical end of the liberal spectrum.

The waves of repression which swept the European continent, most dramatically in the years following the pan-European revolutions of 1848, meant that sustained popular organisation over decades was an almost impossible achievement. Movements oscillated between existing primarily in the space of popular memory, hidden traditions and clandestine conspiracies on the one hand and sudden outbreaks of mass engagement on the other, threatening the state and usually calling down severe repression.

Labour and workplace organising too was a complex and difficult process, dogged by periods of illegality and repression, capable at times of gaining a strong presence in individual, usually skilled, trades. It was not until the rise of the new mass unionism in the late nineteenth century, around the same time as the new mass parties of the Second International and the generalisation of other forms of mass working-class self-organisation, that trade unions could exist as stable, well-established organisations with professional staff lasting over decades. Indeed, as readers of Michels and Max Weber no less than of Luxemburg and Lenin know, they might become so stable that they were barely capable of moving any more.

THE MANY MEANINGS OF 'PARTY'

Up until this period – the 1880s or 1890s in most countries – 'party' did not mean anything like a disciplined body of deputies elected on a single ticket and answerable to a single organisation. Before this it usually meant faction or tendency, as in the *Manifest der Kommunistischen Partei*, which declared paradoxically that communists did not form a separate party in any organisational sense. The *Manifesto* was commissioned from Marx by a small organisation of radical migrants emerging from clandestinity and excited little interest until official condemnation of Marxism as the supposed inspiration of the Paris Commune, two decades later, convinced activists across Europe that there really was a spectre haunting Europe and it was a Marxist one.

The variety of different organisational forms in the early Second International (in particular around the relationship between parties, trade unions and state power); the post-World War I split with Lenin's Third International and its very specific organisational model; the development of Trotsky's Fourth International; and then the postwar mutation of the French or Italian communist parties into popular subcultures while those in the Soviet bloc or China became organs of state power – all of this is, or should be, familiar to those who now assert from a supposedly Marxist standpoint the centrality of 'the party' as though the two words were a definition rather than a question.

From the transformational moment of 1968, however, the meanings of 'party' have changed again. Communist parties had long degenerated into institutions of brutal power in the Soviet bloc and China; in parts of India (or South Africa after 1994), they had become part of the ruling apparatus. Social Democratic parties and the US Democrats were already well on their way to becoming 'catch-all' parties; while electoral radical left parties outside these traditions were squeezed into spaces of marginality. In Mexico, the 'Institutional Revolutionary Party' killed three to four hundred protesting students in that year.

Most importantly, though, the long 1968 was primarily a revolt *against* parties: the parties of orthodox Stalinism and its successors in the east, the parties of orthodox social democracy in the west and the parties of national-developmentalism in a country like Mexico. If there is one thing which marks out the revolts of that year from earlier revolutionary waves, it is this scepticism towards existing party forms. The subsequent creation of new parties – from the International Socialist Organization to Die Linke, from today's Sinn Féin to Syriza and from the Greens to Podemos – remains in practice a (contentious) exploration of this question rather than a simple assertion of 'the party'.

This is not only a west European, or 'global North', question. It is equally and far more a question of what happened to 'the party' as a central form of state power under Stalinism, including the last major survivor of the period, the Chinese Communist Party, as well as those in North Korea, Vietnam and Cuba. And in the majority of the world, it is the question of the disappointments of popular beliefs in the state and party forms associated with independence and postcolonial national-developmentalism.

In the run-up to independence and the decades immediately following, parties such as the Indian National Congress, Mexico's Institutional Revolutionary Party, Ireland's Fine Gael and Fianna Fáil, South Africa's African National Congress and many more were able to secure long-term power as the institutional form through which a movement became a state. They combined a genuine capacity for mass mobilisation with state power and a programme for some economic redistribution combined with industrial development, despite the very different periods involved: the 1920s for Mexico and Ireland, the 1940s and 1950s for much of Asia and Africa, the 1990s for South Africa. Today, it is not just the *credibility* of parties which has been burned away by these experiences of failed popular hopes; it is the question of what 'the party' actually means in practice.

'THE PARTY' IN THE TWENTY-FIRST CENTURY

I am arguing two things. First, in the labour and peasant movements, in national-democratic and anti-colonial movements and for that matter in religious and fascist movements, parties were often an integral, even the dominant, part of movements. (Sinn Féin members still talk of 'the republican movement' today.) Unions, journals and newspapers, and the other organisational forms now identified with 'the left' *as distinct from* movements were an integral part and parcel of this historical period, which is broadly speaking the moment of 'organised capitalism', between the rise of sustained mass organisation from below in the late nineteenth century and before World War I, via the highpoint of the welfare state compromise, state socialism and postcolonial national-developmentalism, to the crisis of 1968 and the turn, sooner or later, to neoliberalism in all of these contexts.

Second, the dominant aspect of these forms became intimately associated with state power in different parts of the world – as social democracy, official nationalism, Soviet-type states and so on – so that after the collapse of this period we have seen them maintain a zombie-like existence, ever more closely associated with neoliberal politics – whether European centre-left parties, India's CPI(M), the ANC in South Africa or the Chinese communist party. As Tomás MacSheoin pointed out in response to an earlier draft of this book, if movement-linked parties once set out to capture the state, it is at least as true to say that the state wound up capturing the party. Movements need to learn from this experience: not necessarily to reject parties per se, but to think seriously about how and in what way parties can actually further movement struggles.

Partly as a result, the bulk of popular movements in recent years have preferred to invest less heavily in hopes of a new kind of party. In the west, the radical and minority form of this kind of left has all too often continued in existence *without* any sustained relationship to popular movements, using the party form as a means of its own organisational survival but at the cost of an institutionalised separation from popular struggle, attempting in different ways to intervene from outside. I say this not as criticism but as observation, because it helps us to understand the difficulties involved better.

Today we do see a handful of cases where this is not the case, and it is worth noting *how different* they are one from another: those South American contexts where radical parties, far more organically linked to popular movements, have taken control of the state – themselves varying from Cuba to Ecuador and from Brazil until 2016 to Venezuela; Anglo-American experiences of trying to infuse the existing Labour and Democratic parties with movement content via Momentum or Bernie Sanders and European explorations varying from Syriza to Podemos and from Die Linke to the Pirate Party.

'THE PARTY' AS A QUESTION

Once again, 'the party' is a question – notably, its relationship to social movements; and many of the experiments just mentioned, from Greece to Bolivia, have seen severe conflicts with social movements. If, in many countries, traditions of popular struggle feel well and truly burnt, exploited or betrayed by political parties, the first response of a left worth any respect should be to take that position seriously and listen to it. Only then, as I will argue, to ask how the left can contribute *positively* to movement development and building real counter-power.

Nothing is less helpful, in this complex and contradictory context, than to insist on the unproblematic meaning of 'the party' and to expect others to agree, after this long and difficult history, that 'the party' is self-evidently the way forward to systemic transformation. Party members do not, after all, always have much to show by way of evidence for this belief. In many countries, movement activists can reasonably observe that their efforts have tended to bear rather more fruit than those of radical parties. Hence, the aspects which convince party members and around which they build their own identities are not the only, or even the main, things that other activists think of when they hear the word 'party'. In this context, neither defensiveness nor attacking other activists who are expressing a very widespread historical experience are serious political strategies for those who aspire to lead popular struggles for change.

Part of the difficulty is the primacy of internal politics on the left. In moments of political defeat – which the neoliberal period in general was up to the rise of the anti-capitalist 'movement of movements' from the late 1990s on – the organisations which survive and persist tend to be those which invest most heavily in *internal* identity formation and organisational maintenance. Those which are most open to the wider world tend to get pulled apart, or co-opted, as happened notably to those green parties which once expressed feminist, ecological and antiwar movements that had radically challenged state power on a very large scale. On the Marxist left, and especially in the English-speaking world (itself increasingly dominant culturally in the neoliberal period), a belief in 'the party' became defining of what it meant to be 'a Marxist' as against 'an anarchist'. At one time, different variants of Marxism were further defined by allegiance to a specific model of the party, which remains the case notably within Trotskyism.

In recent years – particularly in this same Anglophone world where there is no real memory of a large-scale Marxist party, whether of the French, Italian, Soviet or Indian kinds – we are seeing a new kind of contentless nostalgia for 'the party', innocent of any sense of this history. It has become a symbolic marker of radicalism to attach hammers and sickles to logos, or to joke about airbrushing and gulags, as though these things never had a real meaning. (Self-identified 'tankies' may well have little or no idea of the origins of the name, in the Soviet invasion of Hungary to put down a popular uprising.) It goes without saying that this represents something of the sheer unlikeliness of such movements ever achieving state power; but it also represents a very un-Marxist refusal to learn from our own history – as well as a barrier to serious solidarity with movements in majority world countries and elsewhere where orthodox, Soviet- or Chinese-aligned parties exist as oppressive and exploitative parts of the system rather than as part of popular struggle.

There are material reasons for this new contentlessness. If we think further about the real organisational meaning of 'the left' in most countries today, we are far from the older situation where the typical left intellectual was a paid organiser, writer or politician directly accountable to a left party or union. Much more commonly, today's left intellectual exists within 'traditional intellectual' relationships: of the university, commercial journalism, publishing and the media. To assert themselves within this sphere *as left intellectuals*, they need to commodify certain kinds of identity marker and develop a sort of left celebrity status. These are real organisational relationships, with different practical effects in the kinds of relations they create between the intellectual and their audience, what these two positions ask of one another and what kinds of communication they privilege.

An important aspect of this last point is a new politics of opinion, visible not only on social media but equally in the kind of argument which seeks to assert one's political identity by celebrating *this* and condemning *that* – rather than, in a more political mode, finding ways to build *alliances across difference* and support the more radical tendencies within one's own context. Indeed the politics of opinion, particularly as manifested in the online space, is a politics which is not about convincing other people to do things together; it is a politics of asserting one's own identity by attacking others for the benefit of an audience.

The left variant of this is no better, and no less a form of identity politics, than what it condemns under that name. It is not only in its moralising forms, but equally in its 'more radical than thou' forms, that such a politics of pure opinion is actively destructive to any chance of building counter-hegemonic power – which depends precisely on listening carefully to what other people say about what they need, how they are organising and where they want to go, and then trying to build links which help to advance the process; as Marx put it, 'In the movement of the present, they also represent and take care of the future of that movement'.

Where parties have been willing to listen, remarkable things have happened, as in the two most dramatic present-day revolutions. In Mexico's Chiapas, a Marxist-Leninist group aiming at a conventional kind of revolution made contacts with indigenous activists and discovered, as they put it, that they had been resisting colonisation for the past five hundred years. The urban leftists had the good sense and humility to listen to what the peasants had to tell them about this resistance and existing movements in the region. The ensuing Zapatista movement, driven from below with decisions made by all participants and foregrounding indigenous and women's struggles, has been able to defeat the Mexican state for nearly quarter of a century.

In Syrian and Turkish Kurdistan, the authoritarian communist PKK remade itself substantially in the 2000s as its imprisoned leader Abdullah Öcalan read the writings of the US anarchist and social ecologist Murray Bookchin and its cadres reflected on the failures of their original strategy. In the extraordinarily difficult conditions of the Syrian civil war, the Rojava region has seen an autonomous, grass roots-democratic popular revolution, working across different ethnic groups. The feminist dimension of this revolution has become dramatically visible in the women's military units fighting against ISIS and the Turkish invasion. Effective contemporary revolutions, then, offer some strong empirical support for the proposition that parties which are willing to *listen and learn*, rather than propose eternal truths, may contribute significantly to genuine popular rule, ethnic liberation, the defeat of capitalism and patriarchy.

MOVEMENTS ARE ORGANISATIONALLY COMPLEX

In a broader perspective again, *all* of the things we have been discussing – left intellectuals, radical academia, alternative media, political parties, trade unions, but also credit unions, community organising, solidarity economy, NGOs and so on – typically have their origins in social movements. There is then – for all of them – a serious question both over whether they can still be considered as part of movements, but also the question of whether it is worth making the attempt to take them back, in whole or in part.

This argument is very familiar in relation to different forms of labour struggle: can we, should we, fight within existing trade unions, given the long-term history of most actually existing union organisations? Are they irredeemably ossified and incorporated within the system? Is there scope – as well, or instead – for new forms of worker organising? And if so, is the question primarily one of how to support new emerging forms or does it make sense to actively carry out missionary work on behalf of (for example) social movement unionism or whole worker organising?

If we think in this way, *across* this whole organisational range, we are asking a much clearer political question. On the one hand, there is a long history of popular struggle generating new and creative institutional forms, which have inflected large parts of society in many different ways, and (on the whole) positively. If none of these forms existed today, there would be little hope indeed. At the same time, many of these forms seem to be thoroughly co-opted by the institutions of neoliberal capitalism, the nation state and cultural conservatism, while some have colluded deeply in repressing popular struggles. Understanding this paradoxical dialectic helps us to see both the ways in which movements from below have helped make the modern world, and the ways in which movements from above have reshaped our movements and what were once their institutions.

Strictly speaking, then, the question is not one of movements versus parties: it is one of whether a particular party, or party form, can still be considered a real part of social movement struggles, or if it represents something else, a 'gathered church of the elect' standing above and apart from those struggles and condemning their theological failings. In fact, this question goes for the left as a whole.

WHO IS 'THE LEFT'?

The unqualified phrase 'the left' is beloved of subeditors for precisely the same reason as it is useless to help us think. In a subtitle, 'The left must . . .' or 'The left's problem with . . .' works well precisely because it is a fudge, an empty signifier into which everyone can read whatever suits them best. It should be fairly obvious that in most countries today, and especially in the US and UK, there is no 'real' meaning of the left in (to put it baldly) the traditional Marxist terms of concrete political organisation. Nobody would seriously argue that we have a present-day equivalent of the French Revolution's Assemblée in which one could identify those deputies sitting on one side of the room and radically opposed to the power of church and king as 'the left'.

Instead, there is a constant *practical* question: if within society (whether within parliaments or opinion columns) there are forces which can be said to represent that same general tendency but in our present circumstances, what are they? There is therefore an argument, first, as to what we include on the left. If we grant – as we usually do since the later nineteenth century – that it must include not only radical-democratic but also socialist (in the sense of anti-capitalist) visions of the future, do we also grant that feminism, anti-racism, LGBTQI, disability activism and so on belong there in the same way despite their conservative wings? After all, there are also right-wing radical democrats, conservative trade unionists and one-nation socialists.

Second, do we feel that 'the left' necessarily relates to a particular force in society – or even, is it defined by such a relationship? Marx was wary of the term 'socialism' in 1848 precisely because it represented a programme of the radical middle class. More specifically, does the left have to have concrete social points of reference (working-class people, women, ethnic and racial minorities and so on, who are often the same people in practice) – and, more threateningly for the neoliberal centre-left and a certain kind of radical intellectual – does it have to have some structures of democracy, participation, accountability, dialogue, collaboration and so on that structure this relationship? In other words, is 'the left' in whatever form a transcription into some more public articulation of *social movements*? Or does it stand in glorious isolation from these?

Third, *where* in society does this left exist? In the early twenty-first century, it rarely exists in parliaments – not so much because of active repression in most countries (despite some vicious exceptions like Turkey and Russia) but rather because we have returned to the late nineteenth-century situation where the left may have some relationship with liberal forces in the official public sphere but largely exists outside of these. Certainly, we cannot talk of 'the left' in a parliamentary sense in anything like the way one could even fifty years ago, on the eve of 1968.

In fact – as the preceding discussion has hopefully shown – some of the liveliest debates are not really about the political vision of the left, or even about the proposition that the left *should* have some kind of active and two-way relationship with popular actors, but rather about what organisational forms best express this, today. This debate, I would suggest as a student of social movements, will be won in practice by those who develop the most effective and sustainable organisational forms for the conditions people are actually trying to organise under, rather than by those who argue loudest (and often against all the evidence) for the universal suitability of their particular model.

TWO DIMENSIONS OF THE LEFT

We can think about this in two ways. First, from a historical point of view, 'the left' as it exists at any concrete point in time represents something like an archaeological sediment of movement history, a combination of more or less fossilised forms that once helped to shake empires and force capital to organise redistribution and provide welfare, as well as many individual elements of this history – particularly intellectuals, theoretical traditions, periodicals and small organisations – which have taken on a life of their own, for good or ill. (As with language and culture, so too in any political tradition we often practise and justify given ways of doing things as an identity marker, with little real idea of where they have come from.)

The left is thus only in part made up of people who have entered the left from movements. It equally includes people who have entered this left directly, in its discrete forms (today often via social media or the university), and are only aware of its roots in this longer movement history to the extent that they learn about it through sectarian circuits, reproducing the many blind spots particular to that specific tradition. This is one important reason why many people think of 'the left' as a sort of Platonic entity, existing prior to and even against actual popular agency.

Second, however, what gives 'the left' real life is that in one way or another it *includes* – although it is by no means restricted to – the best of many movements. Many people, having become involved in movements, come to see a wider picture and come to feel the need for some form of theory, organisation and vision which goes beyond that particular experience and connects multiple struggles – over time, across space and between different social groups and conflicts.

This is, incidentally, the vision Marx presented for his imaginary communist party (faction) in 1848: a coming together of the most determined, most insightful and most strategically minded activists from the struggles of the day. Comparable visions have been conjured up by many since: from Gramsci's idea of the party enabling a proto-hegemonic alliance between the most conscious elements of urban workers, the rural poor and for that matter intellectuals (under working-class leadership), to some of the best radical left and left-green visions after 1968 of a 'social movement party'. To mention these different histories is at once to indicate a sense of the common challenge, but also the vast differences that lie between them.

It is also worth noting that this 'party' role can be carried out within an anti-authoritarian framework, geared to the coming together of grass roots struggles which do *not* seek to have a common line or electoral programme, but rather seek to find what could be called their 'highest common denominator' in the same process of mutual radicalisation that goes together with movement development in general. As in the nineteenth century or under conditions of clandestinity, it is important not to fetishise electoral politics or ideology as defining what a 'party' is.

From a Marxist point of view, as I have argued elsewhere, the real question is not whether 'the party' is a good or bad thing for movements *in the abstract*, separate from any consideration of the level of movement development or the concrete organisational nature of a specific party. Rather, a party is a good thing for movement development precisely to the extent that it actively contributes towards connecting previously separate struggles, bringing large sections of these movements with it in a real process of deepening political consciousness in ways that arise organically out of movements' own needs and learning processes, and in this way helping what Lukács called 'the point of view of totality', of the whole social order, to become visible and contested in ways that are connected to real social agency rather than an abstract idea.

This is the programme which I and others have articulated as one of 'learning from each other's struggles': one in which the basic position is not one of a separate elite judging popular movements and approaching them in an instrumental way, but rather one of activists involved in different ways in the many different learning processes that go on in social movements, who come to understand their own needs, struggles and visions more clearly in the encounter with each other.

For members of 'the left' who do not come from this process, the challenge – if they are serious about actual popular agency and do not just seek organisational reproduction as a goal in itself – is to engage in this dialogue constructively and, if they have nothing specific to offer in terms of their own social experiences and struggles, to help transmit learning from other generations and other places in ways which help to build links of solidarity and to deepen strategic thinking.

Movement activists often need this learning and understanding, when it is presented as part of a dialogue of equals and a contribution to their own struggles. If people do not have a personal, family or community background in struggle, it can be a huge effort to reinvent the wheel, whether in terms of tactics and strategies, making links beyond an individual issue or beyond a single place, and perhaps most fundamentally seeing the structural and interest blockages that stand in the way of genuine systematic change. The necessary arguments over the boundaries of a movement and its relationship to other movements – the development of a bigger picture and deeper alliances or the choice to ally with elites in return for limited local concessions – are shaped by this learning. The left has much to offer in this context.

RECLAIMING THE LEFT

The challenge is then to overcome the historical alienation of the left, the extent to which it has become an object originally produced by movements but now standing as separate and often opposed to them. This might be a double movement, both (as suggested above) a movement of people who come from the left and learn to understand their own knowledge and practice more deeply as the sedimented product of earlier popular struggles, and to translate it back for present-day generations and through processes of building alliances and solidarity – and one of social movements coming to reclaim 'the left' as their own terrain, if necessary against the career celebrities and the bureaucrats, or rather against those who choose to prioritise organisational reproduction and their own internal status over everything else.

'The left', in this vision, is what survives, beyond the struggles of the moment, of the work of popular movements, deformed by the conditions of defeat and marginalisation, co-optation and commodification, academicisation and routinisation in which the institutions and traditions produced by movements have had to try to survive. In order to continue *as* a left, it needs the constant, life-giving encounter with the process of movement struggles, learning and development and the constant inclusion of new people shaped in this process.

Part of what defines moments of political advance is that they are times when, far from the left being primarily constituted of survival mechanisms, it is transformed by this encounter with new people and experiences. When movements remake not only the party, but also the radical press, trade unions, the left academy, NGOs, left publishing, popular memory, community organisations, alternative media, popular art and all the rest of it – these are also the moments in which popular movements make history beyond this point and become able to imagine transforming the whole social order in line with their own practices and visions.

If we are not in a moment of political advance today, we are certainly in a moment of organic crisis of the social order. This doesn't just mean the 'morbid symptoms' of the different ways in which competing ruling-class factions attempt to define ways forward for themselves. The corruption and soft coups of a Temer or a Zuma, the religious right movements underpinning a Modi or an Erdoğan, the tightening grip of a Xi or a Sisi, the sabre-rattling of a Putin, the spectacle of a Trump or the witlessness of Brexit: these all represent more or less desperate experiments, on the part of ruling classes which are no longer able to continue ruling as they have done, or whose populations are no longer willing to going on being ruled as they have been.

The challenge in this situation is to see if and how far *our* movements are capable of constructing an alternative way out – which doesn't mean primarily the creation of a 'vision', in the sense of a party manifesto, a think tank report or a cookbook for the future, but the construction of alliances of popular movements with a clear identification of the opponent and a serious attempt to act as challengers for the power to shape society. If we are already active within existing institutions connected to movements, our job is then to see if we can help to make them work *for* movements in this period, rather than remaining self-referential organisations focussed primarily on their own reproduction: can we 'reclaim, recycle and reuse'?

I hope it is clear, then, that this chapter is not intended as an attack on particular organisations or even an 'if the cap fits, wear it!' Rather, it is intended to encourage activists organised in parties, radical periodicals and other 'left' projects to keep asking themselves seriously if those projects *do* contribute in real ways to the development of movements, and if they are growing and learning from their engagement with movement struggles.

Conversely, of course, it is also an encouragement to activists and organisers who identify primarily with a particular struggle to consider how far their movement organisations reach beyond themselves to make allies, to generalise the struggle at a higher level and to understand the structure they are resisting more deeply – and to ask themselves how they can contribute to sharing what they have learnt from their own struggles with new generations of activists in other movements, other places and (as history and age catch up with us all) other times.

Chapter 4

Practice-Oriented Thinking: 'The Philosophers Have Only Interpreted the World'

In 1986, I had just arrived in Norway as a school exchange student, only to discover that Maggie Thatcher was coming to Oslo. Thatcher had a lot to answer for: support for apartheid in South Africa and for Ronald Reagan's brinkmanship with nuclear weapons in Europe, war in the Falklands and deaths in the jails and streets of Northern Ireland, hostility to gays and lesbians and brutal police violence against the miners and New Age travellers alike. Despite having read about the latter, never having experienced any of this on my own skin, I still instinctively trusted the police.

The demo in Oslo was big and cheerful, marching through the town. At a certain point, a group of radicals from the Blitz squat broke into the courtyard of the castle where the state banquet was happening. Despite their aggressive rhetoric, the Norwegian police had proved incapable of defending a mediaeval castle against an unarmed demonstration. With much of the march, I went into the courtyard to chant slogans outside the dining hall. The police made up for the embarrassment of letting us get in by filling a gateway with tear gas and using horses, dogs and batons to drive us out through the gas. It wasn't a pleasant experience, but thankfully that was all there was to it (for me: others were injured and arrested).

Being physically attacked changes your perspective in a way that reading about (much worse) things happening to other people does not. I know, in the classroom, that many students from conservative backgrounds will assume, no matter what, that the police are in the right. If someone is hurt or even killed by police, they will say, it must have been their fault. Conversely, those who have grown up in communities which the police treat as enemies find it much easier to look at the actual facts rather than respond with blind trust. These fault lines have recently become very public in relation to Black Lives Matter in the US and protests in Paris around police violence. What struck me most strongly, in Norway, was talking later the same evening to a trade union official who had not been there but assured me that the police were in the right and had given us warnings. I had had no warning before being attacked, but here was someone much older unable to accept my eye-witness experience.

In the previous chapter, I challenged a version of politics which is organised primarily around opinions and parties and separate from movements, experience and practice. In this chapter, I want to go a bit deeper into the kinds of learning that develop through collective practice in social movements and the kinds of action-oriented thinking that flow from these. Gramsci talks about a contrast between 'good sense' – thinking grounded in our own situated experience (as subjects of violence or cultural stigma, as women or ethnic minorities, as workers or LGBTQI people) – and 'common sense', officially approved ways of thinking which (for example) assume that those in authority (or in uniform) are by definition in the right, which disbelieve stories of racist discrimination or sexual assault, which automatically side with managers or the dominant culture. 'Good sense', though, is not simply this kind of experience: it is also what we learn from it, how we interpret it and what sort of action and practice we decide to engage in on this basis.

A PRACTICE-ORIENTED MODE OF THINKING

There is a constant temptation, in academia and on the left among other places, to see other people, fundamentally, as things rather than agents, and to read off their present and future movements from their structural situation as though only 'we' (with the bird's-eye view) are able to analyse and act, while 'they' (down there, in the mud) are only able to react to their immediate context in predetermined ways. This temptation is, perhaps, strongest in English-speaking countries where the legacy of Thatcher and Reagan's defeat of popular movements runs deepest, where Trump and Brexit have replaced the 'progressive neoliberalism' of Obama and Blair, and where nostalgia without history – the desire for a kind of mass radical left party that never existed in these countries – leads radical academics and leftists alike to simulate this past while in fact existing within a strange kind of commodified intellectual celebrity. Even here, in the belly of the rough beast, alternative ways of being are always available – learning from the actual relationships with movements that many such radical intellectuals do maintain – but they come at a cost to the ability to knock out the sort of talks and tweets, articles and books required for this kind of role.

But 'they' – as we discover if we stop and listen to other people who are often better activists than us – are no less able to think and act for themselves than we are; often more so, in terms of the greater challenges they face in their own lives and their greater ability to see the constraints they are under. We do not, ever, find cultureless human beings, people without an understanding of their own needs, individuals who are not thinking about how to make life better for themselves and the people they love.

When I got my first job, teaching care workers at a technical college in working-class Waterford, I had been an activist for well over fifteen years, abroad and in the Dublin left. I had done my time in direct action, political parties and stuffing envelopes. I had studied a lot of political and movement theory and felt pretty confident that I knew about most of what mattered in Irish movements. In particular, I thought I 'understood' what the problems were between the left and the working class in Ireland.

In Waterford, though, I met working-class community activists for the first time, and discovered that – like indigenous communities in Chiapas – working-class Irish people had been effectively organising themselves and asserting power on the ground, beneath the radar of 'the left' and academic research, for decades. Here was a mass movement, grounded in some of the poorest communities of the country, structured around grass roots self-organising, with an extensive programme of popular education, its own media and largely led by women. Two decades later, community activists would face down the state in estate after estate across the country, preventing the installation of water meters, boycotting payment and forcing a major political crisis. None of this could have been predicted from either the academic or the political literature, and in fact such communities in other west European countries are rarely organised in this way. We cannot deduce from people's structural situation what they will actually do.

PLACING AGENCY IN THE CENTRE

When we actually *research* popular struggle rather than taking it for granted, we find people shaped by the legacy of past struggles just as we are: past victories which have come to form new kinds of prisons, past defeats which have left certain possibilities seemingly closed for ever, past traditions of thought through which people articulate their new ideas and strategies, past forms of life which shape what they think they want. And as we research and take part in these struggles, we find people struggling through the contradictions within themselves and with each other to shape new ways of naming what is wrong and how it works, who 'we' are and what we want, how we are going about it and what might be possible.

When Alf Nilsen and I wrote *We Make Our Own History*, we limited ourselves to trying to articulate the theory of social movement implicit within

Marxist theory and practice, not because we felt that class relationships and class struggle were the only significant dividing lines or modes of theory, but because it actually took a book just to do this and to get beyond the traditions of top-down structuralist Marxism. In a series of email exchanges, ecofeminist Ariel Salleh and I argued this out.

Ariel (rightly) noted that there is not only class but also gender, race and ethnicity and our relationship to the natural world. Where to my mind Ariel (and much of this tradition of thought) went wrong is to argue for placing multiple forms of *structure* at the centre and then attempting to deduce radical *agency* from this. As the past forty years of this kind of exercise have repeatedly shown, when you do this what you usually get is a valuable but deeply minoritarian form of radical academic theory, these days far more distant from debates within the movements it celebrates than (for example) 1970s socialist feminism was from the struggle for paid childcare or 1980s ecosocialism was from the struggle against nuclear power.

The point is that if determinist forms of Marxism were wrong to read off working-class consciousness and agency from 'the objective situation' of 'the working class', the problem with structuralist determinisms cannot be resolved by adding yet more determinisms, because actual popular agency and consciousness are not passive and mechanical things but active and creative processes. There is certainly a *relationship* between large-scale social structures, individuals' situation within these, how they think about it and what they do about it – but that relationship is not only complex and contradictory (which is grist to the structuralist mill), but also processual and dialectic – constantly changing as movements challenge and are attacked by their opponents, merge and split – and irreducibly about *popular collective agency*.

In this sense, the 'post-structuralist' tradition and similar approaches remain prisoners of the structuralist logic developed by Louis Althusser as an in-house theorist of French Stalinism. Structures and discourses are still treated as real and human agency is not, however complex the set of prisms through which this is viewed. This is one key reason for the weakness of much academic theory in terms of political practice: because it continues to emphasise structure above all else, it naturally falls either into despair (the structures leave no real place for effective resistance) or overoptimism (oppressed people resist, and this is enough in itself). Either way, the only real choices are moral ones, not practical ones.

And yet 'politics matters'. Not because of the 'bird's-eye' article of faith that the systemic level, The Party or Theory, where the top-down intellectual imagines themselves to sit, is the most important place which determines everything else – but because the ways in which people understand their own struggle, and how they decide to develop it, and what happens when they encounter other actors, from above or below, are absolutely decisive to the outcomes: this is also, incidentally, an important reason why activists like to argue about things. From a Marxist point of view, you can describe the external world any way you like and convince yourself and a handful of your colleagues or comrades; but what counts is the unpredictable ways in which hundreds of thousands and tens of millions of people understand their situation.

If there is no master key to the universe, no *reductio ad absurdam* in which we would finally combine all the relevant axes of inequality and structure within a single orrery (as Thompson wrote of Althusser's system-building) and set it moving in the most perfectly convincing way, what can we say about movements that responds to this primary fact that they are movements and not things, people and not objects, actors discovering and inhabiting their own agency rather than pawns to be moved about on a hypothetical chessboard?

HOW MOVEMENTS DEVELOP

We Make Our Own History attempted to draw out some of what the Marxist tradition – and not only the Marxist tradition of thinking about class – had to say about how movements develop. One reason for starting from Marxism is that it is perhaps the best developed *movement-based* tradition of thinking about how popular agency works. In particular, as Rjurik Davidson recently noted, a long history of defeat reminds us that neither analysing exploitation and oppression nor celebrating resistance is *enough*. The path from either to actually defeating the structures in question is a very rocky one; and Marxist thinking on movements has as often as not been a reflection on why this process did *not* happen, and what might work practically to do better next time. This is not to say that similar discussions never happen elsewhere; and we strongly encouraged others to carry out a parallel exercise and try to 'reuse, reclaim and recycle' other movement-based traditions of thinking about agency.

A conversation between *these* – 'what can we learn from each other's struggles, and from what each other has learned about struggle?' – would be, I think, the first real step towards an integrative theory. Of course, such conversations exist: they took place in many different ways around the traditions that led from the Zapatistas' mix of indigenous politics, socialism from below and women's liberation via Peoples Global Action to the summit protests around the turn of the millennium, and in a more polite and orderly form through the World Social Forum process, for example. To the extent that we are now better able to work together than before, we have learned something; even if it is not always evident quite *what* we have learnt, and in moments of defeat the merchants of old certainties on the left and in academia have done their best to substitute their tried-and-true strategies for the actual process of popular learning-in-struggle, and with little honest discussion of how effective their own strategies have been in the past.

In our analysis, Alf and I started from 'local rationalities', the logics by which people attempt to make good lives for themselves in situations not of their own choosing and with the cultural inheritance of the past. These situations are fundamentally shaped by power, economics and culture; but the hope for change here comes from the 'good sense' of people's practical engagement with external reality as opposed to the 'common sense' perspective within which hegemonic forces seek to encourage them to react.

At times, movements erupt when these local rationalities are squeezed to the point of no longer working – when forest guards prevent Indian indigenous populations from carrying out basic subsistence tasks, or when meters for commodifying water start to appear outside working-class Irish homes where people are already turning to moneylenders to pay the bills. At other, more hopeful, times people sense an opening in power relations and attempt to extend their existing local rationalities – for example, gay and lesbian relationships – into a wider arena and seek legalisation. Such 'militant particularisms' are particularist because they always start in specific places: with the dykes, trans people of colour and sex workers of Stonewall, with already-radicalised estates in Dublin and Cork, or with Bhil Adivasis encountering radical activists from the cities – but they push beyond everyday normality.

They then have to be generalised, in what we call a 'campaign': whether by appealing to others as lesbians, as Adivasis and so on or by appealing to others around an issue like water charges, gay marriage or whatever. Often, of course, those trying to develop a campaign by linking up existing militant particularisms and others who are not yet in active struggle try to do both: to name both an issue and who the 'we' are who are going to fight for it, including the allies we hope to win to our cause.

TOWARDS A SOCIAL MOVEMENT PROJECT

Such a campaign does not, of course, change everything: and this is true *not only* (as left critics of identity politics complicit with neoliberalism note) for newer kinds of struggle *but also*, and over a much longer history, for working-class struggles, which have typically been incorporated in various ways into existing regimes. Conversely, at other times, *all sorts of issues* have provided the basis for transforming the social order: race, ethnicity or religion in independence movements; gender and sexuality in defeating religious patriarchy; class in producing welfare states or state socialism; and so on. What produces this kind of 'social movement project' is precisely going beyond a single campaign to a challenge to the entire social order. This can be contained in almost anything: salt (India), shoes (Burma), rent (Ireland), bread (Russia), and the list goes on.

It is *not the issue* or even the language which determines this: it is the extent to which movement organisers are capable of making alliances with others *so that* a specific struggle comes to be a struggle over the shape of a whole society, nationally or on a larger scale, so that participants and opponents alike understand that the symbolic issue speaks for a whole alternative vision of the social order in which we articulate our good sense against their hegemony – not only their cultural rule over us but more importantly the whole system of social alliances involved in hegemony.

Often, as in the current resistance to Trump, those who seek to develop such a social movement project out of the alliances involved are at loggerheads with those who seek simply to instrumentalise it for a return to conservative Democratic Party power and a continuation of progressive neoliberalism. Neither the issue nor the opponent necessarily determines the outcomes of such internal struggles, which are normal in any significant social movement – however attractive it is to imagine that they are all we need to know in order to understand everything.

But if we are capable not only of articulating a vision but also of having that vision represent the active participation of many different powerful movements in the attempt to construct a different social order, we can bring about an 'organic crisis', a breakdown of existing relationships of hegemony and a situation in which the ruling class, as Lenin puts it, can no longer go on ruling in the way it has been doing, in which ordinary people are no longer willing to go on being ruled in the old way and there is a huge increase in popular self-activity, or in his words 'independent historical action'.

Such a crisis creates a situation in which agency is at an absolute premium, and this is clear even in those moments – like the Diggers and Levellers in the English Revolution – where movements' chance of actually winning was small. It was the depth of the crisis of 1917 that gave an individual, even an extraordinary political operator like Lenin, the chance to transform the situation by creatively bringing together the struggles of urban workers forming soviets, deserting and mutinying military units, peasants taking the land, the Petrograd Soviet and the (often equally recalcitrant) Bolshevik Party – not his own individual genius. It was the crisis of imperialism that placed small groups of intellectuals, artists, revolutionaries and writers in a position to shape future independent states and societies by bringing together peasant movements, working-class struggles, religious revivals and the self-creation processes of the urban middle classes.

... AND AGENCY?

It will be seen that there is a certain logic to this process; as Thompson noted, there is still a chain connecting these things, however deeply buried. However, it is important to see that it is *not* that we start and finish with class (or anything else): rather, as in the very title of Thompson's *Making of the English Working Class*, the subject ('we') and the issue are constructed in the process of struggle, in ways which cannot be foreseen and moreover which *change* as a movement develops. No successful movement *ever* created an organic crisis around one issue alone.

National independence, to take one of the movements which had most success in remaking societies in its own image, always depended on bringing together a *multiplicity* of actors and convincing them that defeating colonialism would advance their own struggles. Indeed one of the questions to be resolved was whether the postcolonial future *would* be one of nation-states. In the late nineteenth- and early twentieth-century Asia (where over half the world's population lived and live), this was not so obvious, and pan-Asian Buddhism and pan-Islamicism were among the alternative answers to the question. By the 1920s, not least after Irish independence, matters were rather clearer and a new nationalist middle class was only too willing to take over the reins from its colonial masters.

Independence also included, necessarily, a conflict *between* these actors whose outcome is also not predictable in advance: in China, against the backdrop first of its subordination to Western power and then of Japanese imperial expansion, the class element prevailed, particularly in the countryside, and the result was a dramatic transformation of the standards of living of the Chinese poor, structured around a massive land reform in particular. In India, as Subaltern Studies has documented extensively, popular struggles were internalised by the nationalist movement but ultimately to the benefit of the national bourgeoisie and urban elites. In Ireland, the success of peasants in becoming small landowners *before* independence led to a state in which landless labourers, women and workers were effectively subordinated, and largely contained ideologically within the Catholic nationalist project for several decades.

Thus, the apparent essence, the core structural relationship, around which movements are constructed turns out not to manifest in any simple way in the process of struggle. It is misleading to imagine 'the working class', as a pre-existing entity, coming to a full and accurate understanding of its own situation *as given in some book accessible to intellectuals*, and on this basis elaborating an action which inscribes this new self-understanding on the world: that may do at times as a useful shorthand, but it is not how the process works. Nor – to avoid the risk of misunderstanding – is this more true for gender, ethnicity or any other social relationship; and yet it remains true that these social relationships are central to struggle and the processes the French movement theorist Alain Touraine summarises as I-O-T: Identity (of the movement), naming an Opposition and articulating a project of Totality.

While agreeing with this analysis, it is important to note that 'Identity' is constructed around real relationships, which are *already* multiple (the Russian Revolution, for example, was started by women workers and saw major ethnic clashes). How the enemy is named has to be plausible in terms of people's concrete *and multiple* experiences of exploitation, oppression and cultural hierarchy. And the vision of totality has to work for *multiple* 'campaigns' (in our terms) which are brought together in a social movement project. There is no automatic transmission belt from structure to action. People have to experience structural relationships and interpret them for themselves (often in collective and contested ways); they have to work out how to respond, usually in dialogue with other people in the same situation and learning from mistakes and defeats. We cannot abstract from this process: or rather, all attempts to do so have failed.

WHEN MOVEMENTS DON'T MOVE

Leaving aside the academic arguments, and moving to activist reality: the single most common experience, as we all know, is that movements don't always move. People necessarily have local rationalities, ways of coping with their practical living situation which attempt to meet their needs; yet these do *not* always erupt as militant particularisms – indeed, local powerholders if they are wise will do their best to prevent this happening; and it is often the action of more powerful, less local forces which disrupt the equilibrium that has been successfully keeping the poor in their place.

Militant particularisms break out all the time; and yet few of these become sustained campaigns tying together different local struggles and bringing in new, as yet unmobilised groups. When they do, it is more likely that they will be defeated, or incorporated into a fundamentally unchanged social order, than that they will ally with others to develop a large-scale social movement project. At all these various levels – subordinated local rationalities, contained militant particularisms, co-opted or defeated campaigns – we are talking about what actually constitutes 'normality' in social life, what it means that things fundamentally don't change and that people become cynical about activism and respond with bitter resentment to the suggestion that things could improve. Routine sociology, anthropology, political science and so on set themselves the task of describing precisely this situation: what happens when people stay in their place, when struggles remain local or when issues are managed within 'the system'.

Of course, our most bitter experiences – less often chronicled in research – are those of the defeats of social movement projects and the failure of movements to win through in situations of organic crisis. These highlight the crucial fact that not only do movements not always develop, but that even at these levels they can be defeated, disaggregated and pushed back into the boxes their participants were struggling to escape from. Intense repression is a routine part of this; but defeat can also take place through the co-option of leaders and organisations, through opponents' success in preventing others from mobilising, or for that matter through the 'dull compulsion of economic relations', everyday power relationships and cultural normality, which leaves others unable to seriously conceive of joining in effective resistance.

What determines how this process goes is the dialectic between actors: the ability of movement participants to mobilise others, radicalise their own organisations, create new and effective forms of struggle, find allies in other places and around apparently different issues and win out in moments of decisive struggle – along with the behaviour not only of outright opponents but of possible allies and others who might or might not join in a conflict. This cannot be neatly deduced from abstract principles, however sophisticated.

It is all too easy to describe movement struggles with the benefit of hindsight and announce that this or that outcome was *always* going to happen. In practice, the actors – including the opponents – rarely know themselves which way things are going. This is true not least because the definition of what the conflict is, what the stakes are and who is involved is itself a subject of struggle, from below and from above: in this sense, there is no 'objectively existing' struggle of which the real, lived struggle is simply a Platonic shadow. As between neurons and theoretical concepts: there is a real relationship, which probably structures something of how we think, but it is an illusion to think that by more closely specifying the workings of neural pathways we can arrive at an ideal theory of theorising. This is the mistake of mechanical materialism – or, more bluntly, of arrogance.

Furthermore, movements from below often make their move not when they think victory is inevitable but rather when they think a concrete gain has become possible, and sufficiently likely to justify the risks and costs. Consider the situation of activists in the Arab world in 2011: if they did not act now, they were certain of another few decades of vicious authoritarian rule, so this might be the only chance they had to unseat their rulers. Conversely, regimes typically mobilise their forces at the point where elites have become frightened enough that hardliners can convince other elites to support repressive action that runs the risk of disrupting everyday consent and legitimacy, but when it is not clear that they have already lost. 50/50 situations, as Raymond Williams puts it, are normal in this context.

THE ABC OF ACTIVISM

If politics matters, this is not necessarily in the sense of states and parties, but in the sense of the dialectic between different social forces. How people constitute themselves collectively as social actors – how they define 'we', how they attempt to make alliances or exclude others; how they understand their situation, elaborate their goals and develop strategies; how they construct their organisations, work within their networks, carry out actions and operate in crises – all of this making and remaking of collective actors in alliance and opposition to one another *matters*.

Thus, instead of a predictable sequence of struggles which could in principle be predicted by a sufficiently finely tuned orrery (or perhaps a sufficiently elaborate computer simulation) we have a space of struggle in which thought and action *count*. In fact, the analysis outlined above is in many ways a rewriting of what I have called the 'ABC of activism' from its original praxis-oriented mode into a descriptive and analytical mode.

The ABC of activism consists of the basic practical principles that enable movements to develop while resisting pressure from above. It can be found in many good activists within the Marxist and other traditions (and in a sense makes up the good-sense cores of those traditions) but activists continually work out these principles for themselves: they are not the private property of any political tradition.

The ABC starts from pushing for more self-reliance in movements, and a broader discussion of the issues geared to wider popular mobilisation as against reliance on the wealthy and powerful as allies or leaders. We are then (initially) in a position of relative weakness, but trying to speak to those not yet involved, a far wider group. It then calls for connecting different movements and issues, which is often the best way to radicalise the focus, and making alliances with groups in other countries working on related issues so as to become less intellectual prisoners of our own context. The ABC encourages engagement with new popular mobilisations and learning from them, again widening out our theory as we widen out our practice.

Along with these movement development tasks, we need to resist pressure from above – in the first instance, all sorts of attempts at demobilisation, co-optation, division and repression. Experienced activists need to try to foresee opponents' likely next moves in this direction. Last, experience also pushes us to look for new possibilities, chances of detaching particular groups from the opposing alliance as well as thinking about possible future crises that might create opportunities to take things further. It will be seen that the ABC is not a 'line', in the sense of fetishising a particular form of organisation or a position on a given issue; but it is a style of organising which is readily recognisable and widely shared by good activists from many different traditions.

THINKING ABOUT REAL POTENTIAL

Perhaps the most important question for activists, both in day-to-day action and in the larger moments of struggle, is what I want to call real potential. By this, I mean the following: Social movements are necessarily about *movement*, not simply rhetorically but practically. People are attempting to change their situation, in smaller or larger ways. In order to do so they need to change themselves (form movements), defeat their opponents and bring those who were not previously allies on board. They are therefore *constantly* trying to do something new: if not always to "do what's never bin done . . . win what's never bin won", then certainly to do what the specific actors involved, in that time and place, have not yet successfully done.

Conventional sociology and social theory struggle with this fact, for obvious reasons. If we accept the usual rhetoric of positivist empirical research, what we look at is what actually exists, and this is what we can research. (Quite how this enables us to have the wisdom of hindsight which we deny to movement actors at the time is another, and rather embarrassing, question in this context.) But undeniably, movements exist, persist and develop insofar as they are able to put their finger on something that doesn't yet exist, and create it.

It is true that – as any sane activist knows – not everything that somebody *believes* might be possible actually *is* possible. I recall with deep affection a ten-day occupation of a university building in Dublin: after the students' union had negotiated relatively successful concessions from the college, a group of good friends decided to stay on until capitalism and the state had come to an end. Knowing they were not going to win did not diminish my admiration for their courage and moral seriousness. And yet, often enough what new generations of activists bring to the struggle is precisely *not* having learnt that certain things are impossible: reaching out into a space that may have been unreachable for previous generations but now *does* exist.

So the concept of 'real potential' indicates that which is capable of existing, not in the abstract but within the immediate future, immediate in the sense of being shaped by our actions, hence within our reach temporally and spatially. (Of course the scope of 'immediate' is then itself also a question of the same kind: our actions have greater or lesser resonance in different contexts.) To be useful in the practical sense I am talking about here, 'real potential' needs to be something which activists are capable of grasping, intuitively or through analysis: in other words, it needs to be *indicated* by something in the present, be that an expression of discontent, a way of acting, a sudden mobilisation for what seemed doomed to be just another dozen-person event, a sudden weakness in opponents or whatever. (This also means that it should be accessible in principle to academic analysis.)

To borrow from the dialogue between social movement theory and the radical Russian psychologist Vladimir Vygotsky, 'real potential' is something like his 'zone of proximal development' in learning theory: it is what we are capable of moving towards, but collectively rather than individually. We both know and do not know it, in that we are capable of imagining the possibility of moving into that space and of becoming the agent who does so successfully, but we are not yet there. In the language of Gramsci and Wainwright, 'real potential' is part of the articulation of 'good sense' or 'tacit knowledge'; in other words, we know it because it is to some extent embedded in our actions, experience, understanding and relationships – but not yet fully.

As activists, we can come to the activist ABC from various points of view: it can be taught formally (or read in a book); it can be caught by association with experienced activists or in a movement which successfully embodies it in its practices and habits; we might simply have the kind of personality which lends itself to this kind of transformative bringing-together of difference. But to use it *successfully*, rather than automatically, we also need a sense of real potential, of when a group, a network, an individual or an organisation is capable of taking a particular step and when they are not. We need this because we cannot fight every battle, and we need movement-*internal* allies who take us seriously if we are to convince others to take a step into what for them is the unknown.

Formal learning, experience and personality can all play a role; but regardless which of these we have going for us we can always *listen* more, literally and figuratively, to others. I say listen rather than watch or pay attention, because listening has a more open, expansive quality. As a traditional Buddhist text on mindfulness notes, it is too easy to have the attention of 'a cat watching a mouse on a dunghill' – with a tunnel vision focussed only on what we want and a predetermined outcome. We need a more appreciative and multidimensional listening in order to hear what potential strands of present-day reality can be brought together to create something new.

HUMAN ACTION AS A WAY OF THINKING

Sticking with the example of Marxism, far too many Marxists, in parties as well as in academia, attach themselves to the letter but not the spirit of Marxian analysis. There are institutional rewards, of many kinds, for becoming adept in different kinds of Marxology, focussed on the precise interpretation of individual texts and concepts, but also for forms of class and historical analysis derived from Marxian models but which are still fundamentally 'contemplative' (Gramsci's term) in form – indeed, Gramsci is increasingly approached the same way despite his more explicit and sustained opposition to this kind of thought. Exactly the same is true for feminism, for ecology and so on: this process is the natural tendency of traditional intellectual activity, and it would be amazing if it did not dominate, even within kinds of theorising which set themselves against the stream in terms of their content.

I want to suggest that what is most transformative in Marx's thinking, and most radical in these other modes of movement-derived thought, is the systematic translation from *propositional thought* – description, analysis, explanation – to *praxis-oriented thought*. In particular, what I mean here is the ability to see not only what is happening in the world but also to explain it in terms of who is doing what, to see what real potential for action exists in or beyond the situation and to make proposals for action which speak to real actors in a credible way.

This does not exclude moral outrage – but it always asks *who* is capable of changing the situation and has an interest in doing so, and *what action* on their part and that of others would be needed to bring this change about. It does not exclude structural analysis and explanation – but it always returns them to *social action*, usually collective, whether exercised through institutions and routines or through movements. This is the cast of mind that Marx describes as 'this-worldly' in his early polemics against the philosophers, and it is what is most fundamental in his class analysis.

To recall, the original point of Marxian class analysis was not to describe the world but to change it. More specifically, it was to identify which social groups have not only an interest in changing the world fundamentally but also the capacity to do so – a point often forgotten in analyses which highlight only the most oppressed without asking about what is needed for their action to be successful, and thus trade any chance of future success for individual moral rectitude in the present.

The question is then, in Marx's own political writings, how specific groups have learned to think about their situation, who they have traditionally allied with, what their history of defeat and success is, their characteristic modes of organising and for that matter how they collude with power: for example, his conclusion that the English working class was too entwined with colonialism in Ireland to be able to transform its own society without forming alliances with the then-stigmatised Irish migrant workers, overcoming their own racism and resisting 'coercion' in Ireland.

Praxis-oriented thinking, in other words, means a concrete examination of the real potential of a particular group of actors. This is what we do in other ways when we try, for example, to bring together a 'feminism of the 99 per cent' as against a corporate feminism; when we try to encourage a local group resisting a particular project to ally with other groups on related issues rather than fighting for local privilege; when we push leftists to take other issues than class and state on board in a substantive way, not as mere tokenism; or when we argue for taking anti-racist struggles beyond an attempt at inclusion on liberal terms and towards a more radical interconnectedness.

AGITATING, EDUCATING, ORGANISING

This cast of mind is one of the most powerful medicines against the gravitational pull affecting most radical intellectuals in neoliberalism: turning ourselves and our movements into simple tools for analysis and description, producers of viral memes and best-selling books, defenders of our own positions and resigned analysts of the way things are. In every moment when we consider the social world, we need to do so with *this* understanding that it is produced by concrete actors in alliance with others; that we think about the real potential for transformation, and which actors under what forms might be capable of changing this; and that we continually seek to turn our passive and contemplative emotional responses – outrage, disgust, cynicism, resentment and all the rest – into an analysis that places the action and practice of those on our side, those on theirs, and those we hope to gain as allies, centre stage.

In academia, in activism and in our everyday communication on social media, in public talks, in writing and all the rest, we should always be asking ourselves the practical questions that follow from this:

- Who am I trying to speak to?
- How does the actual form, distribution or context of this speech or writing relate to that audience or audiences?
- What do I want them to do?
- What real potential do they have for understanding this as being in their interest?
- How much sense do I have of how they might hear and understand what I am saying?

One useful set of terms for thinking about these questions has been found in a wide range of movements since the later nineteenth century. This distinguishes between the tasks of agitating, educating and organising. In this perspective, agitating is communication which seeks to convince others that a given situation is unjust and to move them to want to take action around it. Educating is *not* academic teaching in the usual sense but more specifically trying to bring the audience to a deeper understanding of the forces producing a particular situation and hence of what it will actually take to change it. Organising is then the work of bringing people to act together in ways that are likely to change it.

Of course, these forms of speech can all happen within a single talk; but they do not always do so. There is little point, for example, in taking a crowd that is already so outraged by an issue that they have given up their Saturday to stand around in the rain at a demo – and asking them to listen to speakers tell them how important the issue is. Far better to 'talk turkey' about why the issue exists and what needs to be done to have a chance of overcoming it. Conversely, mainstream academics' evident fear that leftist academics will try to recruit undergraduates if given core teaching tasks is based on the fundamental misapprehension that people who are often only just becoming outraged about the world are an effective basis for long-term organising. And so on: more than anything, we need to think *who* our actual audience is and what we want them to do next.

A related way of thinking comes from Eyerman and Jamison's work on social movements and O'Sullivan's on education. This doesn't distinguish between tasks but between different kinds of knowledge: those associated with organising (resistance, 'organisational' knowledge), those associated with educating (critique of existing social structures, 'cosmological' knowledge) and those associated with creating (creation, alternative 'technological' knowledge).

Once again these can be intertwined, but routinely happen in rather separate spaces; and if we are not clear about which of these we are trying to do, we are very likely to get nowhere. Are we mobilising for conflict? Are we producing the new world in the shell of the old? Or are we trying to understand how the world continues to be the way it is – and by implication what it would take for things to change?

These and similar ways of thinking, then, help us to think *politically*, in other words not simply expressing outrage or horror in ways that do not connect with others, but engaging with them as moral agents with their own different emotions and expectations; not simply using new ideas as a basis for self-publicity or commercialisation but as part of the difficult struggle to try to create a different world; not simply seeing structure as a thing but seeing it as produced and maintained by agents and alliances that can be opposed and disaggregated, as well as seeing the potential for disruption present in how people collude with it in routine contexts.

MOVEMENTS-BECOME-STATES

I want to close this chapter with two concrete examples which underline the importance of demystifying structure in relation to movements, and understanding how much of what we take for granted is the product of collective action. To start with my own place: 'Irish Catholic' as a politically nationalist identity developed over the first half of the nineteenth century, following the defeat of the cross-denominational rebellion of 1798, union with Great Britain and the success of the mass Catholic emancipation movement in defeating anti-Catholic legislation.

The devastating famine of the late 1840s, which saw roughly one out of eight million inhabitants starve and another million emigrate over the following decade, was interpreted by the mass of tenant farmers as being due to multiple inheritance, splitting tenancies between different sons. In its aftermath, single inheritance spread; but this started in the wealthier east, not the marginal west where death and emigration were concentrated. Pointing towards the famine thus legitimated a strategy that meant the disinheritance of most sons, a shared policy of concentration which enabled (for 'stronger' farmers) a greater shift towards capitalist production for the market rather than subsistence.

However, family size remained broadly the same. Thus, if previously a family had ten children, of whom five sons could inherit and five daughters could marry out, now only the first-born would inherit and logically one daughter might expect to be able to marry. In a farming society, without access to land there could be no family. The remaining eight siblings were then condemned to emigration or living out their lives as bachelor or spinster 'relatives assisting' on their brothers' farm – except for those who acquired religious vocations and joined the growing army of priests, nuns and brothers policing the sexuality of those who were suddenly permanently excluded from relationships.

It was in this period that Irish Catholicism came to mean above all sexual control; and if we think about the politics of this typical family, we can understand something of the viciousness of a situation which saw some sons and daughters obsessively controlling the sexual behaviour of their siblings on behalf of the first-born son, all seen through a veil of religious ideology. The ensuing 'devotional revolution' saw Mass attendance become the norm rather than the exception and new religious orders largely take over the education and health care of Catholics even before independence. This orientation makes it easier to understand the growing proliferation of 'total institutions' to incarcerate 'fallen women', the epidemic of institutional physical and sexual abuse, the multiplication of industrial schools and reformatories to control the urban poor and the extreme rates of compulsory psychiatric incarceration (by the later 1950s over 0.7 per cent of the *entire* population). In this emerging Ireland, the church became the key institution through which this emerging community organised itself – in very authoritarian ways.

In this context, the Land War of 1879–1882 saw one of the most successful land reform struggles of all time. Within a few short decades after the Land War, the aristocratic landlord class was de facto abolished and replaced by a new class of small property owners, making up something like fifty-five percent of all households in the newly independent state which was constructed on this basis. Catholic Ireland had thus remade itself through these religious and peasant movements even before independence, as well as through the urban nationalist intelligentsia and the revival or construction of 'national' forms of language, literature, music and sport – the latter still one of the most effective ways besides warfare to generate mass engagement with 'nation'.

The resulting sense of what Ireland 'really is' – and who Irish people 'really are' – remains dominant today not only among the small remaining population of farmers but throughout many groups in Irish society. Still today, for very many people, to be (really) Irish is to be Catholic (and settled, not Traveller). This process is different only in detail from much of postcolonial Asia. Postcolonial societies like the Republic can often be described as a movement-become-state, not only in the simple sense that they are the product of revolutions, but also in the sense that those revolutions were built on the foundation of ethno-nationalist movements which replaced earlier modes of anti-imperial struggle. In Ireland, nostalgia for the old Gaelic aristocracy, or 1798's Jacobin republicanism, were replaced by an assertion of subordinate religion and community against the religion identified with the colonial power.

Again as in much of Asia, a successful struggle for independence from empire necessarily brought together a range of different groups and interests, of which some saw their programme win out while other subaltern groups were firmly relegated to the margins once the new movement had its own state. Thus, for example, the late nineteenth-century women's movement split between a pro-imperial wing supporting involvement in World War I, a small pacifist grouping and a nationalist wing. Despite the latter, after independence women were increasingly relegated to the supporting role implied by the dominance of a property-owning religious orientation, and women's rights would be eroded in subsequent decades.

Similarly, substantial labour involvement in the independence struggle succeeded only in convincing the nationalist right of the threat posed by the left: one of the first actions of the newly independent state was to use the army to break up 'soviets' of labourers employed in the creameries. More broadly, the more radical elements within Catholic nationalism – small farmers, landless labourers and 'left republicans' – were consistently and unsurprisingly defeated in the post-independence civil war and squeezed out of political life in the following decade.

The conservative, religious nationalist leadership succeeded in making a state very much in their own image, even if this could only be sustained at the cost of mass emigration. It took economic crisis in the 1950s, re-industrialisation and urbanisation in the 1960s and early 1970s, the revival of feminism (which had broken in the early twentieth century on the rock of conflicting Irish and British nationalisms), together with lesbian and gay struggles and a permissive counterculture, to finally detach significant groups from this hegemony through a growing disaffection from the church and a return of religious pluralism in everyday life. In this context, 'the social issues' – illegitimacy, contraception, divorce, abortion, gay and lesbian rights and the increasing voice of survivors from carceral institutions and clerical abuse – became the main battleground not only for liberals but also for the Irish left, which understood the strategic importance of these conflicts for society as a whole.

Between the 1970s and the 1990s, much of the power of the church was broken in these areas, though the constitutional ban on abortion and church control of schools remain key conflict areas, while popular memory has yet to engage honestly with *community* collaboration with abuse and incarceration. Along with other movements such as environmentalism, this process has been used selectively by liberal elites in a process of 'passive revolution', where the earlier hegemony structured around religious affiliation, small-property ownership and nationalism has been replaced by a new 'cosmopolitan' iden-tification with (white) Europe geared to service-class employees in particular.

Thus, marriage equality could become an establishment issue in 2016, while the struggle to legalise abortion remained for a long time contested between liberal strategies centred on the professional expertise of lawyers and doctors and the search for a national 'conversation', and radical strategies geared to direct action and confrontation. Irish people's identities, then, in all their complexity and change, are shaped by a long history of multiple and competing movement mobilisation, from above and below: if we add that the sketch above largely excludes Northern Protestants, working-class struggle and republicanism, it becomes clear just how much the contested 'we' is a product of collective action.

Such movements-become-states are a normal feature of world history: the construction of a certain kind of state and civic nationalism in the US and France; the insertion of the institutions of the workers' movement into Scandinavian welfare states; the complex relationship between very different workers' and peasant movements and the state that produced the USSR and the People's Republic of China; the various forms of nationalist, religious, peasant and/or working-class movements which turned colonies into independent countries around the world. This much is at once celebrated and forgotten, because any state needs both to justify its origin and to neutralise that origin in ways that exclude the possibility of a future revolutionary transformation from below. The tedium of official ritual, statues, street names and the like is not only a battle over memory in the sense of celebrating a particular version of history; it is boring *precisely* because the point is to take a moment of active popular transformation and turn it into the dead weight of established ceremony.

MOVEMENTS FROM ABOVE

Movements from below can become states and in other ways (co-option, commodification, conservatism) become tools of power, of wealth or of the cultural status quo. But the concept of movements from below also implies the possibility of movement from above. By this, I mean something more than the *political* alignment of a movement on the right, though this is usually at least part of the point: movements from above are forms of collective action which rely on privileged access to the state, to directive power within the economy or to cultural hierarchy.

Thus, for example, racist pogroms depend, in practice, on the state (with its monopoly of organised violence) standing passively by if not actively helping. This is as true of the rise of fascism in Italy as of anti-Muslim violence in Burma. Paternalist forms of liberalism, too, rely on an 'enlightened despotism' strategy to use state power in imposing polite behaviour on social groups they deem incapable of achieving it for themselves, whether in transforming ecological struggles against nuclear power into anti-littering campaigns or in turning the fight for women's rights into the policing of sex workers. The international state order itself, at the extreme, is a form of collective agency in which elites collaborate on maintaining a particular kind of international order as well as jockeying for positional advantage within it (and on occasion trying to reshape it).

Other forms of collective agency are mediated through economic power. Contemporary right-wing assertions of misogyny and racism, hostility to 'political correctness' and threats of violence, are often in practice organised through the concentration of media ownership, joining up people who for the most part have little organising capacity of their own but are happy to act in coordinated ways *in response to* attempts at mobilising from above: the Brexit referendum is a particularly visible case of this. In workplaces, too, many forms of personal self-policing – and the wider kinds of individualist moralising that come out of this and support neoliberal assaults on collective provision – are organised directly as managerial strategies, for example around productivity and performance. Neoliberalism itself is a very powerful form of collective action, operating first through the takeover of national and international economic and financial institutions and subsequently reproducing itself in the same way. Nobody who watched the showdown of the 'Troika' of EU, European Central Bank and IMF with the Greek government over debt in 2015 can seriously doubt the collective agency of the former.

Finally, it is fairly obvious that many forms of collective action are *all about* mobilising a sense of cultural dominance – attacks on the self-assertion of women, gays and lesbians, trans people, racial and ethnic minorities, nomads, the disabled, prisoners, sex workers, drug users and so on depend on this privileged position in cultural hierarchies – or, at times, attempts by groups not at the top of the cultural ladder to assert themselves at the expense of others. Poor whites in the Deep South, TERFs (trans-exclusionary radical feminists), working-class respectability, ethnic minority followers of fundamentalist Christianity and so on all represent this latter reflex.

Of course, movements from above often combine two or three of these. They may also do so in combination with some genuine collective organising from below – they are not all pure astroturfing or manipulation, as historians of the intersection of racism with white feminism, or of conservative labour unions with the exclusion of women or migrant workers, or of patriarchal and conservatively religious movements of ethnic and racial self-assertion from below have shown. However, their character and how they operate is fundamentally marked by this dependence on *power*, on *wealth* or on *cultural authority* in order to organise. This is why the best (unfortunately far from all) of the left tradition has always been opposed to wars and racism and supportive of women's movements, and why the same approach is important in other movements: these things divide us, to the benefit of those who are not on our side.

HOW DO WE OVERCOME HEGEMONY?

Much of what we experience as structure, as power and routine, has to be traced back either to its historical roots in the (often partial) success of some earlier movement and its institutionalisation as a new order, or to the collective agency of the wealthy, the powerful and the culturally dominant, with or without allies from lower down the social order. This can be deeply depressing when we think of the human qualities of those involved, but it also brings matters more within the realm of what can be changed. States have been created in the past and are maintained by complex alliances in the present: the cutting edge of Gramsci's analysis of hegemony is precisely that this can be disrupted, and better alternatives put in its place. This is *because* elites also have to mobilise, and they are just as capable of making mistakes in doing so as we are. Some members of popular groups are willing to line up behind elites: we need to argue with them, show them that this is not in their interest and offer them ways of mobilising that are more in line with their own needs.

Gramsci's arguments drew on his own experience. A bright boy with a disability from an impoverished family in small-town Sardinia, he followed his elder brothers in emigrating to Italy's industrialised North. Here, Northern racism led local workers to fight against Southern (Italian) migrants as less civilised, religiously backwards and undercutting wages; while in the South, peasants traditionally lined up behind the local priest, doctor or other notable to seek immediate concessions while reinforcing local power structures. As a communist activist, Gramsci looked for practical ways of organising both sides differently, looking for ways in which Northern workers could show practical solidarity with the best organised and most independent Southern peasant movements, and encouraging Sardinian migrant workers to work together with Northern radicals rather than supporting middle-class Sardinian nationalism. He tells the story of organising migrant workers to fraternise with Sardinian soldiers sent in to break up a strike: the regiment had to be withdrawn under cover of darkness.

When he was arrested by Mussolini's police, the start of nine years of fascist imprisonment which he would only leave on his deathbed, Gramsci was the public leader of a communist party which had already largely gone underground. Alongside all the organising this implied, he was working on an essay on 'the Southern Question' attempting to lay the basis for developing long-term alliances between the two on the basis of opposition to landlords and factory-owners alike. In the resistance against fascism and after, these ideas and this alliance-building strategy helped to develop a powerful tradition of building alliances between the most radical elements of different movements, with a view to changing the whole society and not simply one dimension.

Chapter 5

Movements and the Mind: From the Streets to the University

In a partly abandoned village in the Catalan Pyrenees is an old farmhouse, recently renovated by a group of volunteers. The Ulex centre is a new training space for social movement activists from across Europe – British people involved in direct action against coal-fired power plants, east European LGBTQI organisers, global justice activists and trade unionists, radical democrats and international solidarity workers. The trainers are usually activists themselves, from a wide range of different movements, and the 'students' are their peers, with lots of experience and ideas to draw on.

Ulex is one among many social movement training projects around the world: some existing as stand-alone centres and others as one-off workshops or regular summer camps; some taking the form of websites, handbooks or online courses; and some forming a normal part of movements' everyday activity. 'Training' is not always very formal: it can be as simple as activists discussing together how well a particular tactic is working, whether a flyer or video will do the job or how to organise a new network – and reflecting on their own past experience.

Wherever you find social movements, though, you will find people passing on skills to newcomers or arguing about what went wrong last time, discussing theory or gossiping about how other organisations do things, writing and publishing, talking and joking, trying to articulate what they already know and looking for ways to take things further. This chapter mostly focuses on how movements' thinking manifests within more mainstream institutions like the university, but understanding these manifestations depends on realising that movements *think for themselves*, in ways that most of us may not be aware of or even recognise as such.

MOVEMENT THEORISING IN 1900s BURMA

One of the leading political figures in colonial Burma was an Irish hobo
(migrant worker) and sailor turned Buddhist monk, known to later history
by his Buddhist name U Dhammaloka. Between 1900 and 1913, Dhammaloka was active across Buddhist Asia from Japan to today's Sri Lanka,
in India and Thailand, Singapore and today's Malaysia, and probably
elsewhere. As a white man who had 'gone native', subordinated himself to
Asian religious authority, and in other ways breached the racial boundaries
of empire (begging, going barefoot, wearing robes), Dhammaloka's presence was a challenge in itself to the attempt to maintain European power
through asserting the cultural superiority and fundamental difference of
whites.

Dhammaloka's main tools included a massive publication effort of a
fairly ordinary kind: cheaply printed pamphlets distributed free by volunteers at large gatherings and strategic locations. But they also included a
very traditional Asian Buddhist means of intellectual production, preach-
ing. His 'sermons' attracted audiences of thousands, in rural contexts often
travelling for days, as well as attracting police surveillance, a charge of
sedition, the equivalent of an extradition request and surveillance by the
embryonic intelligence services. (Dhammaloka was probably comfortable
with this: he had five different names, there are twenty-six years missing
from his biography, and he faked his own death.)

His talks repeatedly stressed that Europeans came with 'the Bible, the
bottle and the Gatling gun' – in other words through Christian missionaries,
through cultural destruction and through military conquest. To each of these
themes there was a corresponding political programme. Temperance activism was safe (if probably ineffective). Challenging missionaries on behalf
of local religion was something the imperial power had to tread very cau-
tiously in responding to. As in Ireland, though, it was no secret that behind
anti-missionary critique lay a critique of the Gatling gun, which could not be
expressed publicly but could be understood by all concerned.

These talks in turn drew not on the traditional Buddhist arguments that
might be expected of a travelling preacher, but on those of radical Western
freethinkers (atheists), lightly rewritten and repackaged for the local audience. From the exchange of pamphlets and newsletters between his Buddhist
Tract Society and American radicals to the Asian Buddhists who organised
and translated his talks, via the printing press and the telegraph, theorising
was a material activity, and the control of these 'means of intellectual production' was central to effective activism – as witnessed by legislation which
sought to restrict access to these in various ways.

INTELLECTUAL ACTIVITY AND SOCIAL MOVEMENTS

The relationship between intellectual activity and social movements is any-thing other than linear. The history of revolutions and popular struggles has moments where the most important discussions seem to be going on in the creative reinterpretation of popular rituals, among artists and novelists, in popular discussion clubs or local organisations, in newspaper articles or in little underground publications, in consciousness-raising groups or after-work meetings, between philosophers or in departments of sociology, in under-ground organisations or in the internationals of radical left parties.

We can safely ignore the belief that a single book, or a single thinker, 'makes' a social movement: this is at best a pedagogical shorthand designed to enable a way into the real debates which were crystallised in a particular individual or text, at worst a self-serving or elitist misunderstanding of the immense processes of collective learning, argument and articulation which then reappear as if fully formed in a single person's brain. It is because Marx or Gramsci engaged so intensively with the movements and ideas of their day that their thought remains relevant today.

Any serious engagement with what is going on in movements demands much more of us, and today a conscious going 'against the grain'. The pages of the mainstream press, the books of radical celebrities or high-status theories within academia – all the places which the contemporary organisa-tion of knowledge presents as the commanding heights of understanding, the 'debates' it is important to 'engage with' – all these are structured in ways that systematically obscure their relationship to movement theories, even when their debt is considerable, because of the particular commodity form required for success in these fields but also the kinds of social relations required to become a leading 'traditional intellectual'.

As sociologists, or historians of past movements, our task becomes that of finding the much less glamorous spaces within which movements actually think and argue about who they are, what they want and how they are going to get there. There is no master key to identifying such places, which shift with bewildering rapidity – from movement-controlled spaces like Indymedia to commercially structured ones like Facebook; from face-to-face spaces like the popular political clubs of the late eighteenth and early nineteenth century to the organisationally linked radical periodicals of the later nineteenth century; from the debates between opposing position papers characteristic of the twen-tieth century radical left to the situation of many recent movements where the 'medium is (in part) the message', in that a particular line is incarnated in a particular mode of organising, from the lesbian separatist commune to Occupy and from direct-action worker solidarity to urban guerrillas.

Thinking about the means of intellectual production can be helpful here. Marx left us with the recognition that 'the class which has the means of material production at its disposal, has control at the same time over the means of mental production'. Of course, his own work no less than that of his contemporaries was an engagement with the real tensions, between writing and publishing for commercial publishers and the *New York Tribune* on the one hand, and on the other writing and publishing in what we would now call left media but at the time were the organs of a radical intelligentsia and a semi-clandestine workers' movement, as in his classic *Civil War in France*, presented as an address from the First International. Indeed as editor of the *Rheinische Zeitung* in the early 1840s, he had close experience of the challenges of dealing both with the liberal bourgeoisie who funded the paper as an organ of democratic radicalism and with the censorship of the Prussian state: small wonder that he noted, 'The first freedom of the press consists in not being a business'.

Almost by definition, in a non-revolutionary situation, the bulk of the means of intellectual production – be they mass media, universities, the Internet, religions or whatever – are going to be in the hands of groups at least allied with the ruling class: whether state or commercial, a clergy or a technical elite. This is part of what defines and enables consent not to this or that issue but to the entire social order. Conversely – something worth remembering when we get too upset about how the state or commercial media portray our movements – this means that most major movements, and almost all revolutions, take place *against* the determined opposition of the media and so on. More interesting than chronicling their attacks on us is noting how and when those attacks fail to gain purchase.

This latter fact is crucial: from the scurrilous Parisian publications that preceded 1789 to Soviet-era *samizdat* (self-published illegal literature), from popular theatre to radical movies, from the pamphlets of the radical Reformation to anti-fascist leafleting in occupied Europe, from sticking up political posters to blacklisted music, or from the underground press of the 1960s and 1970s to today's radical holdouts in the universities, the intellectual means of production are always just as contested as are other means of production.

Within workplaces, the balance of class power, the unwritten rules of custom and practice, the various concessions or losses, forms of worker representation and external welfare, legislation around and against unionisation and informal and illegal workplace struggle are always shifting. Even when a temporary 'truce line' has been agreed following a major conflict, there will always be attempts to outflank it or create facts on the ground, on both sides. The same is true for the means of intellectual production, both the 'traditional' kind (where workplace struggle provides at least an analogy and at times describes exactly what is in play, in the gain and loss of ground in universities, the serious media or in commercial publishing) and the 'organic' means of intellectual production.

For example, the rise and fall of alternative media (print, broadcast and online) and the internal tensions between collective and individual decision-making, between nonprofit and commercial, between movement-oriented and lifestyle can readily be traced in the origins and history of long-standing print publications like *Il manifesto, Libération, die taz, Time Out, Klassekampen* and so on: all with roots in movements and countercultures but with very different trajectories subsequently. More broadly, movements are constantly experimenting with new media – at times, driving its flow. Much of the infrastructure of today's Web 2.0, social media and comments 'below the line' comes from the late 1990s and early 2000s attempts by activists to develop participatory media in the context of the global justice movement: several key individuals moved from voluntary work in one to successful start-ups in the other.

SOCIAL MOVEMENTS AND THE ACADEMY

In thinking about the means of intellectual production, I want to focus particularly on the university, for two reasons. One is that the conflicts here are less transparent than in movement media and movements' own internal discussion and argument processes. This is because the main opponent is not 'out there', whether in police surveillance and disruption or in the distribution and profitability processes that provide a constant challenge to sustaining alternative media, but 'in here', within academia, a ground which we are never, within capitalism, going to fully control but which can hardly survive without us (as workers, including caring workers, but also as administrators, in the encounter with students and – as we shall see – in terms of intellectual creation).

The other reason is that in recent decades the academy often provides something of the equivalent of the mountains to which defeated guerrillas retire – or perhaps, given its tendency towards petty resentments, the exile networks of political refugees. Movement after movement, as we shall see, has washed up in the university, both theoretically and personally; and while many of those exiles or veterans have no real interest in returning to the fray (whatever they say around the campfire or in the pub), many can be won at times or more regularly to new projects.

Academia's international organisation and the presence within it of people tied to many different struggles and issues mean that (if in often very distorted ways) it sometimes plays as important a role in the generalising processes that constitute 'the left' as parties, unions and radical media – but, as we shall see, this is an ambiguous situation. Like cobblers in the eighteenth

century, printers in the nineteenth or for that matter IT workers today, this
is a form of employment in which skilled workers have sufficient power to
be able to take the risk of political radicalism, to have a certain degree of
mobility and independence from an individual employer and to be able to
do a certain amount of thinking on the job as well as diverting workplace
resources to political use.

Nevertheless, for whatever reason we find ourselves within academia, it
is not only a battleground, but also a deeply ambiguous one. Universities,
and education more generally, are major employers in the public sector areas
which are typically the bastions of conventional trade unionism in the global
North but with an increasingly precarised and bifurcated workforce. They are
providers of substantial services which play an important role in the contemporary economy, in social mobility and reproduction, with strongly gendered
elements of care work in the types of services provided; and they are the site
of recurring conflicts led by students, by non-academic workers and at times
by teachers.

All of this is familiar, and an important part of the daily life of radical academics. I am not focussing on this dimension here because, despite all this,
the university is no longer as politically important in most Northern societies as it once was (and remains in some majority world countries). Student
revolts in the global North, even powerful ones such as the recent Canadian
struggle, no longer shake the whole society or have the capacity to do so as
did the Burmese student revolt of 1988 or the student protests of the 1960s.
Arguably, this is because the university is no longer the equivalent of a
cutting-edge industry: it is far more widespread (in terms of levels of university participation) but adds less value (not least in terms of the meaning of a
degree) and is more widely present across society than in the period where a
more self-contained academy was one of the central, and weaker, links in the
production of the future direction of modernising societies and states.

For the rest of society, then, and in particular for other social movements, it
is no longer movements *within* the university that are its most important contribution to the wider world. This is in part because of the widening of third-
level education, meaning that universities are no longer simple concentrations
of future elites as they once were, but also that academic writing is increasingly accessible to a wider proportion of the population. In part, it is because
the decline of movements' own means of intellectual production leaves the
university occupying a sort of stand-in role as a space for the articulation of
radical thought and organising.

I want to suggest that what is most important for movements in the rest of
society is universities as a space where movement-related ideas are expressed
and fought out and where other movements at times can articulate some of
their organising processes. I say this not to celebrate the university but to

articulate a problem: we (movements) do not own this terrain, but traditional intellectuals are very good at appearing to speak for the whole of society, and hence also for 'us'. Our relationship to academia therefore needs to be far warier, not simply on an axis of suspicion versus trust (which leaves things at an individual level) but in terms of seeing the real politics that are in play. No less than when we engage with the state or with mainstream media, we need to think very hard about the power relations involved in these processes. This chapter seeks to do some of this in relation to the kinds of movement-related *ideas* produced in the university – and conversely, how the university relates to movement thinking.

ACADEMIC THOUGHT AND MOVEMENT THINKING

Colin Barker and I once argued that academic research on social movements is in important respects parasitical on movements' own thought processes. This is almost self-evidently the case as far as research methods go, as most social research processes start from not only what actors do but also how they understand what they do and what they say about it. In other words, to research social movements we typically have to talk to movement participants, read what they write and thus try to work out what their action means to them.

We thus find ourselves in different ways working with movements' own theories (not necessarily Theory with a capital T, though that is also important: theorising happens at many different levels). These theories attempt to articulate as well as shape participants' own thinking and action. Furthermore, researchers' thinking is often itself shaped by these theories, whether through personal participation or because they need to start somewhere, and indeed when a new researcher reaches for formal academic theory, which in turn is often explicitly or implicitly dependent on particular ways movements have thought about themselves. The nervousness with which PhD supervisors insist on their students reproducing a *purely academic* (and, as Cristina Flesher Fominaya and I have shown, seriously misleading) history of theories of social movements hides a reality in which movements' own theorising is both constantly drawn upon and rarely acknowledged.

On a much larger scale, however, much of academia has been reshaped by social movements. The long wave of the workers' movement, and the welfare states it conquered or which were produced in order to stave it off, were fundamental to the development of academic sociology, not only in the lives of its major theorists but also in the project of the technocratic/distributive welfare state which lay at the origins of the normal processes of sociological, social policy and geographical research, as well as much of what happens in departments of education, nursing and so forth. Anthropology has been in large part remade, with the tendencies arising from 'governing the natives' and, later, aid as a weapon against communism and anti-imperialism or as a tool for spreading capitalist relations of production deeper into majority world societies, under severe and sustained assault from critics who stand decidedly on the other side.

Within apparently 'traditional' subjects, history has long been a field of struggle between radical approaches which pay attention to popular experience and culture, movements and revolutions, inequalities small and large – and traditionalists who tell tales of kings and battles as seen from within the archives of the powerful and wealthy. In many countries, 'political scientists' and the technocratic study of 'governance' have largely displaced those scholars of politics who paid more attention to Marxist and other movement-based studies of power: but social movement studies is at least as well established in political science as in sociology, and we are now seeing a new radicalism in political theory, not least with the appearance of anarchist studies complementing older feminist, postcolonial, Marxist and radical-democratic approaches.

Scholars of literature may now pay as much attention to the history of literary articulation within nationalist movements and the postcolonial critique articulated from subaltern elements of those movements, or to issues of class, race and ethnicity, gender and sexuality and so forth articulated within literature as to the 'classical' approach to literary studies. Elsewhere, political philosophers influenced by Marxism, feminism, ecology, critical race studies, the call for a global philosophical curriculum and so on struggle against more conservative forces in philosophy. Even in the most unpromising of fields, like economics, we find struggles for a more critical or radical economics or political economy resurfacing after a period of years. Critical legal studies, too, has its own fluctuating organisation alongside uncritical and conservative trends of legal scholarship.

In apparently apolitical fields such as science and technology, too, many of the questions posed are those raised by social movements, most visibly today in the field of ecology and climate change. While many scientists (and some activists) want to present this interest as something arising purely from natural-scientific research, what convinced universities to fund posts and research in this area over several decades has been the rise of mass popular resistance to conventional science and technology. This was not only in very effective resistance to nuclear power, but also in struggles over everyday levels of pollution (not least from cars), megaprojects such as dams and today the fossil fuel or air travel industries. Medicine too has had to face substantial challenges in relation to women's bodies, from contraception through to the politics of childbirth. Globally, it has been forced to respond to (if rarely to acknowledge) bottom-up health approaches in the majority world pioneered among others by Chinese 'barefoot doctors' and other radical health initiatives and engaging with popular opposition to the activities of the pharmaceutical industry.

More broadly still, the left demand to make connections between different issues, times and places, and to understand the historical production and collapse of different social orders, has led to a constant critique of what used to be called 'bourgeois science', an approach to the world that takes the present existence of largely separate institutional fields as an eternal fact and hence explores each one in isolation without asking after the power relations through which it was produced or the struggles which shape it. From interdisciplinarity through radical versions of area studies, from Marxism or feminism as approaches which refuse the separation of fields to ecologically oriented attempts to collectively shape a better planetary future, the structures of academic work are rarely allowed to rest from the pressure to think further and deeper.

I do not want to paint a rosy picture of this conflict. Any radical academic is aware of the daily battles, and constant pressures, working against these different traditions and approaches, of how easily we can find ourselves isolated in our approach and how important solidarity with one another is in keeping these movement-linked questions and concerns alive. What I want to underline is rather, as Galileo is reputed to have said, 'and yet it does move': our movements do constantly put these issues on the agenda and throw up new questions. It is not only in our own fields but also in many others that companer@s whom we have not yet met are struggling in similar ways to us. We can and regularly do find ways of making effective networks that enable us to keep going.

At a practical level, this can be seen in the extents to which it is possible to use or create standard academic forms of conferences, journals, research networks, mentoring, references and so on to support one another. The *variety* of more or less open or coded speech (as well as straightforward attempts to scrub up and pretend to be something else when faced with genuine opponents in positions of power) is indicative of the varying levels of sympathy in different parts of academia: exploring this landscape is a crucially important step for all radicals coming new to the field. (Something almost any activist brings to the academy is an ability to organise things practically which is often sadly lacking in colleagues who have never had to work in unstructured situations, or do things themselves if they wanted them to happen.) Even where people have long since been ground down into resignation or abandoned their own radical goals in favour of a more managerial practice, they are often willing to lend some support to other people's initiatives. There are of course also 'hypocrites who mingle with the good people we meet' and simply instrumentalise their left credentials in the interests of building an academic career. It is part of practical wisdom to recognise such people for what they are.

MOVEMENTS IN THE UNIVERSITY

This brings us to the question of how *personal* trajectories intersect with institutional *structures* to produce different kinds of radical theory. It is of course easier to write a self-justificatory account than to observe how our own theorising and research practice has been distorted by the power relations and organisational culture we find ourselves within; and perhaps this kind of self-critique is only really possible while taking up an intellectual position grounded elsewhere, in movement realities. Still it is surprising that there is not more research on *what happens* when movement activists become professional academics and movement theories reappear in mystified form as academic theory.

To give a concrete example of the latter, university textbooks in feminism may present a spectrum of feminist theories in a form something like 'liberal feminism – radical feminism – Marxist feminism – socialist feminism – black feminism', with reference to well-known authors in each of these traditions. What is less likely to be discussed, though, is the concrete relationship of this theoretical divergence to the political struggles of the 1970s, let alone the question of whether this particular account represents how the conflict actually proceeded *in different countries* – or how it is organised today when, for example, radical feminist struggle has often been absorbed in the running of women's refuges on the one hand and reappeared as strange forms of theology on the other, while lesbian separatism as a practical political project, let alone the kinds of revolution routinely called for in the period, have all but vanished from the agenda.

Our difficulties in giving an accurate account of our own trajectories and the roots of our choice of research themes, theories and methodologies in social struggles are *intellectual* failures: it is simply not enough to present these things as if they appeared out of thin air or were always there – or to present an apparently isolated history of what would then be the 'positive' development of ideas within a taken-for-granted institutional field. They are also *political* failures, in that they mystify the relationship between movements and academia in ways that serve neither our non-academic allies nor our students. We need more serious reflection on the relationship between ideas and social agency in academia, in the form of a praxis-oriented sociology of knowledge: what are we doing when we theorise? And, more sharply, do our ideas reflect actual battles and contribute to these or do they reflect and justify our own situation, relying on the role of 'traditional intellectuals' and hence seeking 'objective' intellectual legitimacy?

THREE KINDS OF MOVEMENT THEORISING

Of the three aspects of movement practice discussed earlier, the *creation of alternative institutions* is particularly poorly studied in academia, not least by virtue of the university's 'traditional intellectual' structure. While certain kinds of imaginary future (technocratic capitalist futurology and 'innovation' studies or theological forms of normative philosophy) are perfectly legitimate within some academic spaces, studies of the slow and painful struggle of ordinary people to remake the world in practice and the question of where this can go are hard to find institutional supports for. There are small networks studying, for example, community organising or solidarity economy, but in the nature of things they struggle to find recognition within the academic mainstream and are often confined to applied or adult education contexts, where they encounter the greater weight of institutional innovation geared to remaking people for the twenty-first-century labour market.

Resistance and organising, my own field, survives on the margins of academia: there are at an optimistic guess five hundred scholars working full-time in social movements in Europe, of whom only a minority have permanent posts or will remain focussed on this field beyond the funded projects currently proliferating in response to the massive movement upsurge of recent years. Matters are somewhat better in the US, but not by much: the Collective Behavior and Social Movements section of the American Socio-logical Association has about eight hundred members, of whom again many will be graduate students and precarious researchers; if one adds their coun-terparts in other fields, the figure is still not great.

The resource section at the end of this book includes a number of dif-ferent approaches to the academic study of social movements: the narrow, 'canon-building' US perspective; overviews from what is now a broadening European mainstream; Marxist and autonomist approaches; subaltern stud-ies and Tourainean analyses; as well as contributions from feminists, labour scholars, historians, cultural studies and wider sociology. It will be seen that despite small numbers, the field is an intersection of many different forms of theorising.

Conversely, *critical analysis of structure* is the meat and drink of much of the humanities and social sciences – at once the greatest gift of social move-ments to these fields (which live, directly and indirectly, from the intellectual contributions of feminists, Marxists, anti-colonial, anti-racist, LGBTQI, disability, indigenous and other movements) and one of the main reasons the rest of the world reads material produced within these fields. I have suggested elsewhere that there is an elective affinity between this form of movement activity and the academy; there is probably also a certain degree of personal affinity, in that those who are happiest, or have the greatest gift for, this kind of analysis may also be happiest in an academic context where the institutions support them to do so and provide a ready audience to hear the results, without the constant pressure to articulate one's analysis with the pressures of the day.

THE PRESTIGE OF STRUCTURAL ANALYSIS

There is, of course, an academic prestige to top-down structural accounts of society which risks being disrupted by any credible discussion of agency; this prestige derives both from the implied or explicit advice to (political, intellectual) elites and from one's self-positioning as above society and able to view it dispassionately and objectively.

The net effects of this kind of 'elective affinity' are readily seen in much radical academic work. For example, the agitational tendency to seek to evoke outrage in describing oppression, exploitation and cultural stigmatisation is now used to add lustre to educational analysis but *separated from* clear analysis of the collective agency, organisational work and political conditions under which these conditions can credibly be alleviated. We also see a moralising, theological tendency to articulate a weak vision of a better world with no serious attempt to reflect on what forms of social movement struggle might be capable of bringing this into existence. This new utopianism is often just as reliant as the old on assumptions of enlightened despotism, routinely seeking to appeal to the powerful to abolish themselves. By contrast, a radical utopianism is that articulated within processes of concrete struggle such as a protest camp, which leaps beyond the immediate struggle to imagine its collective agency projected onto a far wider scale.

This kind of appeal to the powerful and (again Enlightenment-era) belief in reason runs very deep in the academic process. Almost the default form of many pieces of sociological research is geared towards detailing this or that social ill in the conscious or unconscious belief that 'if only the government knew' they would take action – but with no recognition of the fact that the powerful are bombarded with such material and routinely consign it to dusty shelves unless they are forced to take action on it.

Those who have thought a bit further and want to 'raise awareness' about an issue among the wider population rarely consider the questions of *form* in terms of what might actually be accessible and interesting (it will not be a sociological dissertation), let alone the practical question of *distribution* (how can this be effectively channelled through movement networks to people who are willing and able to act on it; or how can mainstream media circuits be worked around in order to get to the right audience as a call for action and not simply another lament for the suffering of the world) or *politics* (what interests underlie the way things are, who has an interest in challenging the way things are, how are they currently organised and what would it take to broaden the alliance to include this issue?)

In other words, there is often an intellectual and moral *bad faith* in the results of this elective affinity. Academic processes fillet out the agency-oriented perspective discussed in chapter 4 and leave us with something for which 'well-meaning' is an entirely adequate description: justified outrage, a moral call for action, even a critical analysis of power – but only a brief gesturing towards concrete analysis of *who* is capable of changing things, *how* this is going to happen and *what* this analysis contributes to that process. The positioning of a certain kind of political philosophy as 'king' thus reproduces much of the situation of present-day European left liberalism: a moralising discussion of 'what should be' devoid of reflection on agency *but* intent on implicitly justifying its own situation and actions.

WHY WE NEED TO SEE BEYOND STRUCTURE

First, a farcical example: in shock at the Brexit referendum, the rise of Trump, racism in Europe and the authoritarian turn of governments like the Indian or Turkish, many scholars have jumped to assert their opposition to populism and the assertion of 'the people' against 'elites'. In so doing, they have aligned themselves clearly with the failed strategy of what Nancy Fraser calls progressive neoliberalism: the technocratic assertion that what in the US was the Clinton-Obama strategy and in Europe the strategy of austerity with a 'human rights' face is the only way to go, and that (against all the evidence) it remains 'democratic', not on grounds of popular consent or participation but on the fundamentally liberal grounds of law, rights, evidence, expertise and so on.

Lost in this wave of clichés are the core reasons for the twilight of neoliberalism: (a) as a strategy it no longer convinces elites that it is capable of meeting their longer-term interests; and (b) it has increasingly lost the consent of large swathes of the population who initially supported it, a situation not altered by the willingness of voters to support such candidates when the alternative is the far right. Indeed, a substantial part of what has undermined neoliberalism is precisely popular movements '*desde abajo y a la izquierda*', from below and on the left, allied in the form of first the anti-capitalist 'movement of movements' from the later 1990s on, and more recently the wave including the Arab Spring, indignad@s, Occupy, Gezi Park, Black Lives Matter or Standing Rock.

This side of the story – the centrality of popular agency of a radical kind to the undermining of neoliberalism – is far more challenging to mainstream academics and journalists. They have no problem with acknowledging the deformed popular agency of far-right voters – indeed, much effort goes into overestimating the significance of older white working-class men who have switched votes from centre-left to right, as against what is usually the much larger proportion of long-term right-wing voters, property owners and better-off social groups in that vote. Popular agency is fine when it is bad, in other words. When it is progressive, it is hard to acknowledge.

... AND WHOSE ARMY?

A more serious difficulty: I have in front of me a very interesting platform for a new project combining research on the solidarity economy in Southern Europe and the global South, reciprocity as a new theoretical principle of welfare and social innovation. The platform discusses in detail the crisis of traditional forms of welfare and seeks to build bridges between political support for traditional welfare-state objectives with new civil society actors working in other forms. There can be little doubt that we need this given the increasing social inequalities brought about by the crisis of the welfare state, and that scholars should work more with people involved in solidarity economy and other projects.

And yet, as a more critical analysis would object, there is no recognition here of the broader picture: that the welfare state did not simply diminish as a result of its own internal contradictions, but has been the subject of massive and sustained assault for some decades now. The real reason we cannot simply paper over the cracks, this analysis would note, is that we have to tackle neoliberalism head-on and reverse the defeats which underpin its power. Otherwise, we are simply putting sticking plaster on a mortal wound. We cannot bring about greater equality by stealth, without challenging those powerful forces which are actively seeking to produce it; and in the desire to include as many different projects as possible, the radical political perspective infusing the practice of solidarity economy in countries like Greece, Spain or Argentina is obscured.

This criticism points to the weakness in relation to social movements (briefly glossed as 'civil society actors' alongside many others) in the platform. However, I am sure my colleagues in the platform would accept this analysis – while noting that the traditional left account is equally devoid of serious strategies as to *how* the welfare state is to be defended and strengthened. This kind of critique, they might say, amounts to attacking existing popular groups who are not only mobilising on the terrain of basic needs and building often extensive networks and institutions, but reviving a tradition of popular self-organisation around basic needs which characterised European societies in much of the nineteenth century and on the back of which (or at times against which) the welfare state was constructed. Not only, they might retort to leftists, are you refusing real alliances with significant popular movements, but you are doing so on the basis of a nostalgia for the past which lacks any critical analysis of its weaknesses or of why many popular groups ceased to support it in 1968 and thereafter. No more than us, they could say, do you have a serious strategy for what popular agency could reconstitute it on a more credible basis.

I do not want to pursue this hypothetical conversation further, except to note that in my view it is not a question of one or other being right. Rather, *both* need a more serious and substantial reflection on the agency implied by their perspectives and on how their contributions are aimed towards developing that agency, including, notably, the practical political questions of what and how they write, where they publish their work, how it is distributed, who reads it and so on.

THINKING AGENCY SYSTEMATICALLY

In the broadest terms, we need to account not just for what are *obviously* social movements (from below) but also collective agency from above, in the production and sustaining of existing strategies of accumulation, social structures and political hegemony. To treat these social constructions as simply given, or as the products of an agentless history, suits the traditional intellectual, apparently standing above society and representing the whole rather than shaped in the struggle of articulating a particular class project – but this does not make it any the more true, simply a more rewarding position to hold.

Discussions of what, for example, the future of welfare states should be *without* discussing the strength of neoliberal forces or the possibilities for labour and other mobilisation, are empirically meaningless, utopian in the bad sense of refusing to think seriously about how what one wants can come to pass. The same is true for critiques in a negative form, for example of racialised structures of power or of everyday images of gender: without a concrete sense of *how to change the thing one is criticising* they are just elaborate theoretical grumbles, PhD versions of shouting at the telly.

To repeat: all too many academics remain in the situation of pre-1789 French peasants, believing that if only 'people' (then, 'the king') knew how bad things are they would be motivated to do something about it, and implicitly addressing themselves to elite forms of agency (policymakers, the mass media, PhD students). This rehashes Enlightenment philosophers' attraction to enlightened despotism as a way of having one's cake (condemning the bad and demanding the good) and eating it (avoiding any engagement with real struggles for change) – and pays no attention to the limited impact of that strategy when it clashed with despots' own interests. In this sense, movements' own organisational debates on Facebook or small websites are actually a far more substantive contribution.

In very general terms, I want to suggest that it is an intellectual and ethical duty as well as a political one to bring systematic reflection on social movements into academic work. We should not treat it as an embarrassing aside, a necessary but uninteresting step in the theory or something to be discussed outside the classroom or seminar room. We owe it to ourselves and others to insist, first, on as serious an account as we are capable of producing of the social conditions of our own knowledge production and distribution, particularly as they relate to collective popular agency – in our own lives, in our disciplinary or other context, in our research practice, in the classroom, in our writing and elsewhere.

Second, we need to look much more closely at the collective agency that is involved in producing particular social formations and resisting or modifying their effects, and not remain happy with hand-waving and often ahistorical caricatures which today pass for explanations of how we got here. Third, we need to think more deeply about the kinds of agency implied by seriously attempting to end particular forms of suffering, by identifying the specific forms of exploitation, oppression and cultural stigmatisation that underlie these, and by calling for better worlds or more minor changes.

If we can do these three things, we are acting (at least in our thinking and writing) as activists within academia. We are also in intellectual good faith, taking our intellectual activities seriously and exploring their real meaning rather than taking the existing cultural routines of our local social context for granted, in ways we would rarely respect in other kinds of social actor. We are also, I think, living our lives more fully and with greater ethical seriousness than if we prefer an unexamined life and the simple reproduction of institutional mechanics.

AGAINST PARTICULARISM

Sharp-eyed readers will have seen how much of what I am saying here in relation to academic life is fundamentally similar to what I have said of the political left. One could say similar things about radical media production, commercial writing and for that matter much activism within social movements which tries to ignore the wider picture. Each of these spaces has its own logics, its own weaknesses and strengths; in each of them, there is a routine tendency towards taking not just the whole institutional sphere, but one's own particular subset of it, for granted. In the process, we go from being the kind of creative agent we once were as activists to becoming prisoners of the situation on which we now depend: for personal identity, for a salary, for the feeling of having an effect on the world.

It is important, then, to avoid the moralising which simply rules one kind of social context out as a space for radical action and ascribes an automatically radical role to another. It does not take much reflection or experience to realise that this simply means exalting our own situation in a way that absolves us from a more critical and strategic approach, while writing others off in a way that blocks off all possibility for alliances. Furthermore, a brief acquaintance with the history of movements reminds us not only that they routinely appear where the intellectuals of the day – *including* the radical intellectuals – did not expect them to arise, but also that those groups which have been confidently ascribed the role of 'most radical' and so on have regularly failed to act as their intellectual cheerleaders have expected. To confuse the recognition that at times a particular group or struggle is strategically central to power relations across a whole society with the assumption that by definition this particular situation always holds is to practice the politics of the stopped clock – and, typically, to abandon the attempt to build alliances and blame others for not doing so.

However, this does not mean that we should not think critically and strategically. It means that in each situation, including our own, it is important to stand outside the routines of cultural meaning-making and ask more seriously what interests are in play, what strategies we routinely pursue, what forms of struggle persist and recur, how people conceive the possibility not only of amelioration but also of alliance and liberation – and to accord the same courtesy to others, meeting them as real equals whose liberation ours is bound up with. There are, *of course*, situations within which the logics of dominant relationships tend to win out and those in which resistance, even radical resistance, is far more routine, and it is important to see this clearly (and not through wishful thinking), if we are to have a clear sense of the 'real potential' of different spaces that enables us to make gains and build our movements.

But it is necessarily a form of particularism, in the negative sense, to fixate on one space to the exclusion of others, and to refuse the strategic question of alliances for transformation. In Marxism, this is the mistake of workerism, the celebration of industrial working-class culture as it is, even when its dominant forms are corporatist, racist and patriarchal. This is the strategy

Gramsci argued against in his attempt to build alliances between Northern workers and Southern peasants, and it is the strategy pursued in its extreme form by surviving orthodox communist parties like the French PCF or Greek KKE, in their glorious isolation as the material bases of the old industrial working class are (often deliberately) destroyed under their feet.

The strategy is no better when it is based on ethnic and racial minorities, however oppressed, or on the advancement of a small group (professional women, white gay men) through alliance with the powers that be, rather than as part of a broader struggle that brings together multiple radical movements which are willing to consider remaking their own worlds and the forms of oppression, exploitation and stigma they themselves have colluded in or ignored.

Particularism is not the peculiar vice of this or that social group or political tendency; it is the gravitational pressure with which our societies' everyday relationships of material life, power and culture – patriarchal and hetero-normative, racially and ethnically hierarchical, capitalist, state-structured, ecologically destructive and culturally routinised – keep dragging our move-ments down to their level and trying to incorporate, co-opt and neutralise the real potential of social movements radicalising as they develop broader alliances and come to offer a practical alternative way of organising society.

Radical academics need to look for struggle taking place across the whole society, and to build broad alliances. This in no way excludes serious reflec-tion about their underlying interests, their existing forms of culture, their inherited traditions of political organising, their strategic capacity for trans-formation or the prospects for a more radical alliance which will necessarily involve some remaking of all of these. In other words, we need to stop look-ing away from the question of collective agency, and stop treating it as purely a matter of personal identity, cultural status or morality. It is all of these, but it is also, and most fundamentally, a hugely complex *practical* question which our movements have been grappling with for centuries, sometimes more effectively, sometimes less. We owe it to ourselves and to each other – as well as to those who grappled with these questions before our birth and those who will have to live with the results of our own struggles – to take it as seriously as possible.

STRUGGLES OVER THE MEANS
OF INTELLECTUAL PRODUCTION

A particular point of strategic weakness in many contexts is the decline or disappearance of earlier radical movements in education. One might expect that intellectuals working within a particular field would turn their energies to learning about past struggles in the field, engage with the most radical conflicts over what that field should mean and what it should be for and strategise for how to bring those struggles to life in the present – but many radical intellectuals do nothing of the sort and at best have a liberal attitude towards their own practice in this respect.

I have lost count of the times I have talked about radical projects in *children's* education to otherwise radical academics and educators and been met either with a blank face or with an impassioned defence of mainstream education. This in a period in which it has never been more closely geared to the needs of the capitalist marketplace, and when the 'organic intellectuals' of management thought have greater influence than the 'traditional intellectuals' of the old high-culture programme. In fact, it is a marker of our difficulties that nostalgia for a supposedly more 'scholarly' past is often the primary form of defence against the new academic managerialism, not simply as instrumental strategy but as deeply held belief.

Discussing radical projects in *adult* education outside of universities, alternative education approaches within the university, different forms of research methodology and knowledge production is not a way to make friends in universities. As with discussing how we educate our children in a world where their personal advancement through academic merit is a major project of university families, popular education is often perceived as an attack on the everyday routines we put up with in order to get on with 'our own' work, considered in the narrowest of ways.

Thankfully there are still many honourable alternatives, both in countries where the legacy of 1968 went deeper in education, and in countries where the present-day crisis has produced new struggles over knowledge production led by students and precarious researchers that go beyond simple redistributive conflicts.

LEARNING FROM EACH OTHER'S STRUGGLES

I have had the great privilege, in recent years, of involvement in some significant projects in this area, which have been among the best intellectual experiences of my life despite their often taking place far from the glitter of more prestigious academic locations. First, I have experienced social movement struggles which had arrived at a certain degree of self-knowledge, able to sustain (for example) their own education and training programmes, their own publications looking beyond immediate agitational concerns to strategic questions, and their own spaces for theoretical debate.

In particular, the alter-globalisation 'movement of movements' saw the *encounter* of these different traditions, not in an academic space (though many radicals from universities took part) but in a space shaped by the need to bring different movements together – in the networking of practical struggles from the Zapatistas via summit protests to anti-austerity conflicts as well as in more infrastructural or reflective spaces like social forums, Indymedia and so on.

In my own university, we were able to draw on this experience and for five years make a further deepening possible for movements through a taught masters' course in activism, aimed at existing activists in a wide range of movements for whom 'learning from each other's struggles' represented a meaningful objective, in a space which gave them some room for reflection outside the immediate crises and organisational work of movements' day-to-day activity. In these spaces, participants were able to ask themselves whether their groups, networks and organisations were really engaging with the challenges they were initially created for or to what extent they had become prisoners of their own organisational 'means' – and what they wanted to do about this. After a period of research usually geared to this question, they returned to their activism (or to carrying it out in a full-time way) on a more effective basis.

This research was typically (but not only) carried out using participatory action research, a research model itself based on movement practice. In this approach, the researcher is usually themselves already a movement participant, asking questions which arise from a group's or movement's own existing questions. Working with other activists in forms that model or directly contribute to the typical discussion, education or decision-making processes for that movement, their research was based on the conflicting understandings and perceptions of different participants and helped to make the situation clearer for everyone while moving towards a more powerful way of doing things and a sharper self-understanding. I still have the great pleasure of working with some extraordinary activists carrying out research masters and PhDs using this approach.

On a more global scale, the journal *Interface* has attempted to bring such forms of radical research, movement-centred theory and education together in an open-access space which treats movement activists as knowledge producers on a par with academic researchers and connects research within different political traditions and academic disciplines, in different regions of the world and different movements, on the understanding that it is both challenging and costly for movements to carry out their own learning and theorising, education and research processes in the middle of action. 'Learning from each other's struggles' is then a strategy that enables movement-relevant thought, grounded in practice, without always having to reinvent the wheel or change direction on a cliff face, as movements too often find themselves doing.

In mentioning these examples, I do not want to suggest that these are the only possibilities or for that matter the only fields of struggle. I do want to underline that we should be discussing these things far more *as politics* and not simply within the contained space of research methodology or educational theory. As with the question of what we write, how it is distributed, how its form relates to different cultures and purposes and what people do with it, so too the question of how we teach and how we research is one of the control of the means of intellectual production. How we struggle and organise matters; so we need to pay close attention to what we think we know about it and how that knowledge is produced and shared.

THE RISKS OF MOVEMENT RESEARCH

In early 2011, one of the first students on our activism masters was occupying a tractor on a small road in rural Ireland where Shell were trying to construct a monster gas pipeline, part of a fifteen-year community struggle. Arrested with another woman shortly afterwards and driven to a police station, her bag – with her camera in it, still recording – was slung into another police car. When she was released and her bag returned, it had recorded police joking about raping protestors, in a context where threats of sexual violence were rife.

The student bravely decided to go public with the recording. Feminists who thought they had been successful in training the Irish police around sexual and domestic violence got a sharp reality check and joined environmentalists and human rights campaigners in calling for a general investigation of the policing of this conflict. The student, however, was subject to a vicious campaign of tabloid journalism and leaks from the police, while the ombudsman treated her with consistent hostility for refusing to hand over her camera – which included her research recordings of activists discussing their strategy.

Attempts at mediation (e.g., having the recordings deleted by a mutually acceptable third party) were rebuffed and the camera was eventually handed over with the recordings deleted. It took well over a year for the ombudsman to finally back down – and, among other things, withdraw threats of criminal proceedings directed at myself and a colleague. Their final comment, on national TV, was a somewhat plaintive observation that people didn't understand that they had a job to do.

The threat of rape by police is not the trivial issue that many people wanted to present it as, particularly in a small rural community under siege from huge numbers of tooled-up police. Nor, from my perspective, was the threat of criminal action which could have cost me my job. Elsewhere, the threat to researchers is even sharper. In 2016, for example, Cambridge University PhD student Giulio

Regeni was tortured and murdered in Egypt. Regeni had been placed under investigation by Egyptian security services because of his research into independent trade union organising; such killings of Egyptian activists are increasing.

The new global authoritarianism threatens social movement research in a wide range of ways. In Turkey, academics who signed a petition calling for peace in the Kurdish southeast have been jailed or purged. In East and Central Europe, politically inconvenient researchers struggle to find work. In India, radical academics fear reprisals from a resurgent Hindu nationalism. In Italy, a student has been sentenced to a two-month suspended sentence for 'moral complicity', meaning her presence during demonstrations she was researching for her undergraduate thesis. In the US, activist journalist Amy Goodman was charged with riot for filming DAPL guards using pepper spray and dogs on activists (the charge, thankfully, was thrown out). A series of otherwise very different states, in a period of rising authoritarianism and challenges from social movements, are clearly trying to see how far they can go – and researchers, like the movements they work on or with, are in the firing line.

RECLAIMING THE INTELLECTUAL LEGACY OF SOCIAL MOVEMENTS

In normal periods, we can never hope to fully control the means of intellectual production any more than those of other production. Nonetheless, we should expect there to be a struggle here as in other forms of work. In periods of organic crisis such as the present that struggle intensifies, as the power relations that keep the owners of production in the saddle weaken within the field of intellectual production and as our collective strength, confidence and creativity grows. We do not know in advance what will, or will not, work; but we should at a minimum support other people's efforts, document our own and try to learn from both.

At present, as this chapter has argued, there is a significant activist legacy in academia which can in part be reclaimed or demystified, in many different contexts. If Habermas called the radicals of 1968 red fascists, we should rather say that the question of what the university, the media, publishing or the arts should be *for* is one to be asked again and again, in ways that are enriched by the collective nature of the question and which connect with the wider world in relation to which these institutions exist. At the same time as we find that some of our own learning and training represents fossilised forms of earlier movement life, we also find an instrumentalisation of movement rhetoric and practices to suit new managerial goals. Critically engaging with both brings our work to life.

As intellectuals – in other words, if we want in any of these fields to be something more than wage labourers obeying the boss – our task is to question the fields we are in and their wider social purpose; to seek to reclaim academic territory for movement purposes that go beyond our own contexts at the same time as we attempt to change power relations and culture within those contexts. This is the same thing we ask of others elsewhere: to fight on their own ground, to reach out beyond it in forming alliances and to ask questions of the ways in which society as a whole is structured. If we do this while bearing collective agency in mind and constantly seeking to develop it, we go beyond being traditional intellectuals, doing our job in the sense defined by academic managers and official expectations. We might start to become, at a minimum, organic intellectuals of struggles within academia, or to develop sustained and meaningful relationships with social movements elsewhere.

Conclusion: What Should We Do?

Lenin's question '*Chto delat*?', usually translated as 'What is to be done?', has more energy and passion to it in Russian than that translation suggests.

What should we do? Having thought about these things, we need to come back to the central question around which all of Marx's work revolves – as does the best of feminism, ecological thought, anti-racist analysis, LGBTQI theory, radical democracy, anti-colonialism, anarchism and the other popular energies which give life to thought. From the point of view of a fully developed human being, what makes these ways of thinking more real and more alive than others is precisely the way in which they speak for real human needs, name the barriers to their development, discuss what is needed to overcome those barriers and ask what we should do, here and now, to contribute to this whole process of our own development as individuals and as a species.

A BIGGER PICTURE

We do have to look elsewhere, outside ourselves and our own lives, to ask how we can take action against the structures, mechanisms, cultures and processes that block our development, stifle our deepest needs, turn our own daily activity against ourselves and force us into trapped and narrow lives. We might, though, need to have a bigger picture of who we are and what our lives entail: to see the ways in which our oppression, exploitation and cultural stigmatisation is bound up in each other's, rather than remaining stuck in a particularist resentment against others whose oppression, exploitation and stigmatisation is configured differently. If we can see ourselves in them, them in us and name the voices of management, of authority and of glamour that set us against one another, we have already gone a long way.

We do this best not in separate thought but in movement practice, as we try to make alliances around concrete common goals that matter to both of us and that point beyond their immediate effects to the bigger picture. The same is true as we try to develop our movements across space, connecting up the many different, but equally specific, shapes our own struggle takes in another part of our own country, elsewhere in our own region of the world and on the other side of the planet. The process of deepening and radicalising our struggles, of generalising and internationalising them, is the best kind of educator.

COMMON SENSE AND GOOD SENSE

As we do this, if we are honest with ourselves and listen carefully to others, we can see two things. One is the many ways in which we collude with one another's oppression, exploitation and stigmatisation. Some of us objectively benefit from particular structures of wealth, power and cultural hierarchy, others less so; but we are all inclined to avoid noticing the structures, routines and assumptions that do benefit us, whether they are those of class situation or background, gender, sexuality, trauma, disability, race, caste, ethnicity, citizenship, religion, cultural acceptability, mental health or 'neurotypicality' – ignoring how the world is for people with autism, Down syndrome and so on.

Hegemony operates in large part through the ways in which those who are relatively poor, powerless or culturally stigmatised – in other words, the large majority – nonetheless accept the 'common sense' negotiated between the goals of those who rule and our own everyday culture; how we trim our needs and thoughts to fit; how we battle with one another rather than with the real enemy; and how we reproduce in our own lives the forms of exploitation, oppression and stigmatisation we have learned in the world. Articulating 'good sense' is also the process of overcoming this 'muck of ages' in ourselves and above all in our practical, everyday relationships with others, in movement activity and outside it. For this reason, there is no social movement, and still less no revolution, without widespread cultural transformation.

The second thing we can see in this process is the way in which we have learned to accept and internalise our own forms of oppression, exploitation and stigmatisation: how we have learned to trim ourselves to fit into a world shaped to suit others. This process goes deep, and it can be the work of a lifetime to unpick it, particularly if we have suffered from serious trauma and abuse in the process. All too often in the history of movements, people engaged in one struggle start to realise that they were also fighting about something else that they had not yet been able to see in their own lives, and start to fight for that as well – for women's rights as well as black rights, for lesbian equality as well as women's equality; for freedom from religion as well as freedom from sexual control, for example.

A life in movement, then, is also a life in which we can expect to be challenged by ourselves as much as by others – and where, bit by bit, we unpick some of the different forms of suffering we cause others and come to free ourselves as individuals in the process of struggling for a wider transformation 'out there'. If the unexamined life is not worth living, then this repeatedly challenged life is a way of being more fully alive: not in the sense of trying to live up to some impossible external ideal of who the perfect moral individual would be, but in the sense of trying to live more fully with ourselves.

COURAGE AND CREATIVITY

In this process, and in the wider process of struggle, courage grows in unlikely places. Sometimes – perhaps particularly if we have come through trauma – courage can mean in the first place being able to admit that we cannot face every enemy right now, being more honest with ourselves and others about our own limits in terms of the physical threats to our bodies, the practical threats to our lives and our families, or the emotional threats posed by confrontation. With whatever different tools help us to handle this, we can sit back a bit more fully into who we actually are (for now) rather than who we would like to be in order to look well in the eyes of others, or of those eyes as we imagine or internalise them.

When we are being more honest with ourselves, though, we can come to find a new kind of courage, that represented in a firm 'Here I stand; I cannot do otherwise'. We know more fully who we are, and what the bottom line in our own lives is in terms of what we must defend, what we must stand for and who we must be. Past the early adulthood sense of immortality and the rush of adrenalin, we become better able to stand our own ground and fight where we are, in our own lives even without great physical bravery or much willingness to stand in the spotlight. We may also, if we live longer, if we have children or work with students, come to find that we accept the suffering and impermanence of life and become more focussed on what our actions mean in practice for others.

With greater relaxation and honesty, perhaps, we may also find greater creativity: we know that the struggle is likely to be a long one and that there will be many smaller battles along the way – and that other people stand in many different and often contradictory relationships to what we are trying to do. This frees us up to be less a prisoner of how particular issues are presented to us by institutional processes or within social constraints, and makes it more possible to step outside those and 'respond to P-K2 with a lob over the net', refusing to play the game our opponents would like to trap us in.

Social movements are extraordinary spaces of creativity, liberating energies that people often did not know they had. Any real large-scale protest sees people develop their own banners, costumes, jokes and bring different parts of their own world into play – but it also sees people find different ways to engage in the struggle. Some of these may be dead ends, but we do not always know until we try what is going to work best, and what once seemed impossible may now have come within the realm of the doable.

Creativity, no less than courage, is our ally in transforming what might otherwise seem like a lifetime sentence to suffering and conflict into a way of living lightly with what are, after all, inevitable parts of life even if they are not the whole.

A BETTER SENSE OF 'WE'

Earlier in this book, I criticised an unreflected use of 'we'. The problem is not that this is a form of rhetoric or ideology but that it creates a false sense of ourselves and of our relationships to others. In movements, we necessarily use 'we' all the time – in fact, in any good movement it rapidly becomes hard to identify who came up with a particular idea or slogan. Action comes out of 'we', talking together and organising together as part of larger conversations with people we may never meet personally but whom we partially and imperfectly bring into our discussions as we consider who we can mobilise and how, what they may be up for doing and what their hopes are for a better world.

A better sense of 'we', in movement action, is one which captures this process as well as possible – both the concrete 'we' in our meetings, networks and events *and* the different social 'realities', as Latin Americans say, that I and you and she and he bring into the room and (for now) speak for, in suggesting a change of wording, different practical arrangements, a new way of doing things or a wider goal. By paying closer and more political attention, good activists also come to hear what isn't being said, to spot who is not in the room and to think about not just what is immediately doable but how far a particular constellation of 'we' can be taken – or what new 'we' it might grow into.

From a better sense of 'we' comes a deeper confidence, as our sense of who we are and what we do is reshaped in this ongoing interaction with others – and as our collective ability to understand and act grows. As movements engage in conflicts with opponents, our confidence can take severe knocks at times, but if we survive the experience we have moved to a different level of possibility and reality in our action.

Confidence also comes from the wider picture: understanding that our struggle *here* and their struggle *there* are intimately interlinked, or (even better) moving to a sense of these as one struggle and one 'we', far more complex and contradictory than any we could find in a single space. Standing in our longer history, too, reminds us of how often the kinds of defeats which today we are finding devastating have been overcome in the past, and helping us to think of our action not from a conservative point of view, as a foolish and risky challenge to an inevitable present, but instead as part of the process of helping a real potential express itself into (forgive the cliché) a better future.

I spent part of my last year in school, when I was supposed to be preparing for exams, sitting in a now-vanished alleyway behind the Dunnes Stores supermarket in city centre Dublin in case management attempted to sneak in deliveries. Eleven young staff had gone on strike, refusing to handle South African fruit. Initially, they knew very little about apartheid or the international boycott campaign, but were following a union decision to join the boycott. As the strike progressed, of course, they learned a huge amount, while South African activists made many connections with them. The picket line brought together labour and anti-apartheid activists, socialists and republicans, peace activists and development workers, older Dublin workers and young Goths. Ordinary shoppers were mostly very supportive: even without knowing much about South Africa, many had worked in Dunnes themselves or had relatives who did, and had good reasons to support those who were challenging management. The strike lasted nearly three years, with many twists and turns; eventually, the Irish government banned South African produce, the first state to join the boycott. Seven years later, apartheid came to an end under massive pressure from inside and outside. In retrospect, the internationalist perspective of these young supermarket workers and the long perspective of the struggle against apartheid were justified.

THEORY AND PRACTICE

I have suggested in this essay that there are serious difficulties with the main tools we have for thinking about the world and our place in it. We encounter these difficulties in 'common sense' on a daily basis but in more articulated form in mainstream media, academia and a certain kind of left. With Marx, but also with a long tradition of thinking in radical psychology and education about what constitutes a healthy human situation, I am arguing that it is *better* for us – in terms of emotional health, our practical interests and the possibility of creating a different and more human world – to demystify what is apparently given. We can then translate it back into human practice, in terms both of the movements from above which have (usually) won out and the struggles from below which have set limits to them, modified the outcomes in ways that are crucial to the possibility of any kind of good life in the present and continue to contest the way things happen to be at present.

Seeing the world we are in as fully constructed enables us to reclaim a clearer sense of our own agency, both as (under circumstances not of our choosing) we contribute to reproducing it – through our activity in the workplace, the social relations of gender and sexuality, racial and ethnic hierarchy, ability/disability and neurotypicality and so on – but also to pushing against these structures and trying to reshape them. It equally enables us to give life to our frustration, suffering, rage or quiet misery in connecting it with meaningful action and with others in those situations we can grasp as related – and to experience ourselves as part of those wider struggles. Rather than ranting online, keeping our heads down or seeking purely private escapes, we can connect up who we are, what we think and what we do.

Finally, this process helps who we are to come into closer focus as these different lenses – of ideas, emotions and practice – become sharper and more aligned with one another. Theory is sharpened by the discipline imposed by the need to connect it with practice, and practice becomes clearer as we seek to articulate its meaning more clearly in theoretical terms. Our own identity, and our vaguer emotions, move into three dimensions in this process. Of course, these are ongoing struggles for as long as we exist within class society, patriarchy, racial and ethnic hierarchies and states; and of course our own processes of self-construction only come to an end with our death. But this side of those dramatic changes, we have the choice whether to be passive in relation to our own everyday activity, thoughts and feelings – or to take an active role in shaping them, with others.

STEPPING OUT

The world we live in knocks us back, constantly. In 1955, William Carlos Williams, writing the foreword for a thin book of poems by a barely known young gay Jew, wrote, 'It is a howl of defeat. Not defeat at all for he has gone through defeat as if it were an ordinary experience, a trivial experience. Everyone in this life is defeated but a man, if he be a man, is not defeated.' We would now change the language but the point – that we are defeated in our actions but not in ourselves – remains crucial. Allen Ginsberg was knocked back many times: by a conservative culture, by his own mental health and in his last years by his dying body. And yet he gathered his energy each time, became more honest about his weakness and put himself on the line more fully, inspiring others to challenge the controlling American normality of the 1950s, helping assert the cultural side of the revolts of the 1960s from Prague to San Francisco, and speaking both to the horrors and the hope of the years that followed.

We may not be poets; but we have to pick ourselves up again and again, for our children, sick partners and aging parents; to keep a roof over our heads and deal with the indignities of work; to handle our own mental health, poverty, sickness and fear. We do this; it is nothing remarkable when we see it in other people but it can demand a lot of ourselves just to get up and go out in the morning, or to actually say something real rather than just keep a stream of light chatter going. What stepping out means to me and to you is probably very different; but I know from my own challenge of keeping going just how hard it can be for you, and vice versa.

So too with movement activism: we do not need to go looking for it, but we need to keep on stepping out of the door and into the street, placing ourselves in the unpredictable situation with our allies which is movement organising, and then in the unpredictable situation with our opponents that is conflict. Often enough, the challenge arises in the middle of daily life and it is really a question of recognising it, thinking politically, and taking appropriate action rather than simply doing what we are expected to do. It is, in other words, the challenge of actually being ourselves in that moment, and not who other people would like us to be.

Notes

This section does not attempt to offer references for every statement made in this book (which would make for a very long bibliography for chapter 2, for example), but simply gives credit where it is due and references for authors or quotes mentioned in the text (other than literary references). The works by Marx, Lenin and Lukács listed here are available free online via marxists. org. Colin Barker's excellent work is available via https://sites.google.com/site/colinbarkersite/home.

Many of the arguments and empirical claims in the book are discussed in greater depth in Laurence Cox and Alf Gunvald Nilsen, *We Make Our Own History: Marxism and Social Movements in the Twilight of Neoliberalism* (Pluto 2014).

INTRODUCTION

Habermas' four pages are 'New Social Movements', pp. 33–37 in *Telos* (21 September 1981). Gramsci's discussions of traditional intellectuals are collected in many sources; the classical place to start in English is *Selections from the Prison Notebooks* (Lawrence and Wishart 2005, original texts 1929–1935). The 'five filters' are discussed in Edward Herman and Noam Chomsky, *Manufacturing Consent: the Political Economy of the Mass Media* (Vintage 1995; originally 1988). The approach to social movements as formed through conflict draws on Touraine, *The Voice and the Eye: An Analysis of Social Movements* (Cambridge University Press 1981) and Mario

Diani, 'The concept of social movement', *Sociological Review* 40/1 (1992): 1–25. The idea of an ecology of knowledges comes from Boaventura de Sousa Santos, *The Rise of the Global Left: The World Social Forum and Beyond* (Zed 2006). E. P. Thompson's arguments about experience can be found in *The Poverty of Theory: Or an Orrery of Errors* (Merlin 1995; originally 1978).

CHAPTER 1: WHY WE NEED SOCIAL MOVEMENTS

The argument about the different parts of our lives that social movements take place in is from my 'How do we keep going? Skills and strategies for movement sustainability' (Into 2011; free online). Oliver James' book is *Affluenza* (Vermilion 2007).

CHAPTER 2: MOVEMENTS MADE THE WORLD WE LIVE IN

This chapter is particularly influenced by E. P. Thompson's pamphlet *Beyond the Cold War* (Merlin 1982; now free online) and Luciano Canfora's *Democracy in Europe: A History of an Ideology* (Wiley-Blackwell 2005). The discussion of historical waves of revolutions draws on Laurence Cox, 'Waves of protest and revolution: elements of a Marxist analysis', available free online. The discussion of 1968 draws on *Voices of 1968: Documents from the Global North*, which I am coediting with Bjarke Risager and Salar Mohandesi (Pluto 2018). For the discussion of working-class self-organisation and the history of the welfare state, see Colin Ward, *Social Policy: An Anarchist Response* (Freedom Press 2000; originally 1996) and Jean-Louis Laville, *L'Economie sociale et solidaire: pratiques, théories, débats* (Seuil 2016). The comments on managerialism in the Soviet bloc draw on George Konrad and Istvan Szelényi, *The Intellectuals on the Road to Class Power: A Sociological Study of the Role of the Intelligentsia in Socialism* (Harcourt 1979). The discussion of 1968's rejection of top-down power is shaped by Giovanni Arrighi, Terence Hopkins and Immanuel Wallerstein, *Anti-Systemic Movements* (Verso 1989); Hilary Wainwright's discussion of how neoliberalism selectively appropriated the movements of 1968 is in *Arguments for a New Left: Answering the Free-Market Right* (Blackwell 1994). On the movement of movements, see Jai Sen (ed.), *The Movements of Movements: Struggles for Other Worlds* (OpenWord/PM Press 2018). Gramsci's discussion of good sense can be found in *Selections from the Prison Notebooks* and elsewhere.

CHAPTER 3: SOCIAL MOVEMENTS AND THE LEFT

'The social movement as a whole' is a free rendering of Marx's 'die soziale Bewegung überhaupt', 'the social movement as such' or 'in general' (letter to Engels, 11 December 1869). On the broader point, see Colin Barker, 'Class struggle and social movement – an effort at untangling' (2010; free online). E. P. Thompson's *Making of the English Working Class* (Penguin 1968) contains both the 'enormous condescension of posterity' discussion and that of the working-class struggle for political rights. For an introduction to Sheila Rowbotham's work, try *Rebel Crossings: New Women, Free Lovers and Radicals in Britain and the United States* (Verso 2016). For Peter Linebaugh and Marcus Rediker, try their co-written book, *The Many-Headed Hydra: The Hidden History of the Revolutionary Atlantic* (new edition, Verso 2012). On Michels, Luxemburg and democracy, see Colin Barker, 'Robert Michels and the Cruel Game' (2001; free online). The 'movement of the present' quote is in the conclusion to the *Communist Manifesto*. On Chiapas, Subcomandante Marcos, *Our Word Is Our Weapon* (Serpent's Tail 2000) is a great introduction. On Rojava, Michael Knapp, Anja Flach and Erçan Ayboga, *Revolution in Rojava: Democratic Autonomy and Women's Liberation in the Syrian Kurdistan* (Pluto 2016). On the situation of labour movements today, Peter Waterman, *The Old Is Dying and the New Is Hardly Yet Born: Questioning the Global Legacies of Labour and the Left; Devising New Languages of Struggle* (2017; free online). Lukács' discussion of totality is in *History and Class Consciousness* (1923; free online).

CHAPTER 4: PRACTICE-ORIENTED THINKING

The quote is from Marx's 1845 *Theses on Feuerbach*. On working-class community activism in Ireland, see my article 'The Irish water charges movement: theorising "the social movement as a whole"' (2017; free online). For Ariel Salleh's work, see her *Ecofeminism as Politics: Nature, Marx and the Postmodern* (Zed 2017; originally 1997). Rjurik Davidson's article is 'Between Como and confinement: Gramsci's early Leninism' (*Marxist Left Review* 14, 2017). With other *Interface* editors, the call to theorise collective agency starting from feminist perspectives can be found in the *Interface* special issue on 'Feminism, women's movements and women in movement' (3/2; free online). The argument against structuralism draws from Thompson, *Poverty of Theory*. Lenin's definition of revolution is in his 1915 'The collapse of the Second International'. The Diggers and Levellers are discussed in Christopher Hill, *The World Turned Upside Down: Radical Ideas during the English Revolution* (Penguin 1991; originally 1972), incidentally one of the few history books to give its name to a folk song (by Leon Rosselson) still widely sung at protests. On subaltern studies, see Alf Nilsen and Srila Roy (eds.), *New Subaltern Politics: Reconceptualizing Hegemony and Resistance in Contemporary India* (Oxford University Press 2015). Touraine's I-O-T model is in *The Voice and the Eye*. Marx's 'dull compulsion' is in volume I of *Capital*. Raymond Williams' 50/50 point is in *Towards 2000* (Chatto and Windus 1983). The dialogue between social movements research and Vygotsky is currently being carried out by some of the best researchers in social movements: a recent book-length version can be found in Brecht de Smet, *A Dialogical Pedagogy of Revolt: Gramsci, Vygotsky and the Egyptian Revolution* (Brill 2015). The (long) Buddhist text mentioned is Buddhaghosa's *Visuddhimagga* (free online; originally fifth century). Gramsci's 'good sense' is, once again, in the *Prison Notebooks*. Wainwright's discussion of tacit knowledge is in *Arguments for a New Left*. The discussion of different types of movement knowledge draws on Ron Eyerman and Andrew Jamison, *Social Movements: A Cognitive Approach* (Polity 1991) and Ed O'Sullivan, *Transformative Learning: Educational Vision for the 21st Century* (Zed 1991). Gramsci's comments on anti-racist alliance-building are in his *On the Southern Question*, written in 1926 just before his arrest and available in various collections.

CHAPTER 5: MOVEMENTS AND THE MIND

Ulex is at ulexproject.org. Marx and Engels' comments on the 'means of mental production' are in *The German Ideology* (1845). Marx's comments on 'the primary freedom of the press' are in the *Rheinische Zeitung* no. 139 (1842). U Dhammaloka is the subject of a forthcoming book by Brian Bocking, Alicia Turner and myself; existing research can be found via dhammalokaproject.wordpress.com. The argument by Colin Barker and myself is 'What have the Romans ever done for us? Academic and activist forms of theorizing' (free online from Into 2011; originally 2001). The discussion of the pseudo-histories of social movement thinking in PhDs draws on 'European social movements and social theory: a richer narrative?' (coauthored with Cristina Flesher Fominaya in our *Understanding European Movements: New Social Movements, Global Justice Struggles, Anti-Austerity Protest* [Routledge 2013]). Nancy Fraser's discussion of 'progressive neoliberalism' can be found in various places, including 'The end of progressive neoliberalism', *Dissent* (2 January 2017). The masters in activism is discussed further in my 'Pedagogy from and for social movements: a conversation between theory and practice', in *Capitalism Nature Socialism* (2017).

CONCLUSION: WHAT SHOULD WE DO?

Lenin, *What Is to Be Done?* is from 1902. The 'muck of ages' is discussed in Colin Barker, ' "The muck of ages": reflections on proletarian self-emancipation' (1995; free online). On trauma, see Steve Wineman's fine book *Power-under: Trauma and Nonviolent Social Change* (2003; free online). William Carlos Williams' introduction is to Allen Ginsberg, *Howl and Other Poems* (City Lights 1955).

Resources

This book draws extensively on my own work in social movements, in particular my co-written book with Alf Nilsen, *We Make Our Own History: Marxism and Social Movements in the Twilight of Neoliberalism* (Pluto 2014). Other than some of my books, all my other work is available free online in several different places: via laurencecox.wordpress.com, my academia.edu site and my university home page.

This section suggests a range of books that showcase different approaches to understanding and writing about social movements. Much of the best work here combines telling a good story with academic analysis and political argument; I have separated these suggestions for further reading between those which should be accessible and interesting to a general audience, those which will be of most interest to political activists and those of most relevance to people interested in pursuing the academic debates – but most of the books listed could easily be placed in more than one of these categories.

MOVEMENT STORIES

Peter Linebaugh and Marcus Rediker, *The Many-Headed Hydra: The Hidden History of the Revolutionary Atlantic* (new edition, London: Verso, 2012).
Claudio Pavone, *A Civil War: A History of the Italian Resistance* (London: Verso, 2014).
Ronald Fraser et al., *1968: A Student Generation in Revolt* (New York: Pantheon, 1988).
E. P. Thompson, *The Making of the English Working Class* (Harmondsworth: Penguin, 1968).
George McKay, *Senseless Acts of Beauty: Cultures of Resistance since the Sixties* (London: Verso, 1996).
Alf Gunvald Nilsen, *Dispossession and Resistance in India: The River and the Rage* (London: Routledge, 2010).

Ramor Ryan, *Clandestines: The Pirate Journals of an Irish Exile* (Oakland: AK, 2006).
Nancy Naples, *Grassroots Warriors: Activist Mothering, Community Work, and the War on Poverty* (New York: Routledge, 1998).

POLITICAL ARGUMENTS

Karl Marx and Friedrich Engels, *The Communist Manifesto* (many editions; free online).
Giovanni Arrighi, Terence Hopkins and Immanuel Wallerstein, *Anti-Systemic Movements* (London: Verso, 1989).
Hilary Wainwright, *Arguments for a New Left: Answering the Free-Market Right* (Oxford: Blackwell, 1994).
Raúl Zibechi, *Dispersing Power: Social Movements as Anti-State Forces* (Oakland: AK, 2010).
Jane McAlevey, *No Shortcuts: Organizing for Power in the New Gilded Age* (New York: Oxford University Press, 2016).
Rebecca Solnit, *Hope in the Dark: Untold Histories, Wild Possibilities* (Chicago: Haymarket, 2016).

ACADEMIC APPROACHES

Colin Barker et al. (eds.), *Marxism and Social Movements* (Chicago: Haymarket, 2014).
Donatella della Porta and Mario Diani, *Social Movements: An Introduction* (Hoboken: Wiley-Blackwell, 2006).
Ana C. Dinerstein, *The Politics of Autonomy in Latin America: The Art of Organizing Hope* (London: Palgrave MacMillan, 2015).
Cristina Flesher Fominaya, *Social Movements and Globalization* (Basingstoke: Palgrave, 2014).
Cristina Flesher Fominaya and Laurence Cox (eds.), *Understanding European Movements: New Social Movements, Global Justice Struggles, Anti-Austerity Protest* (London: Routledge, 2013).
Alf Nilsen and Srila Roy (eds.), *New Subaltern Politics: Reconceptualizing Hegemony and Resistance in Contemporary India* (Oxford: Oxford University Press, 2015).
Geoffrey Pleyers, *Alter-Globalization: Becoming Actors in a Global Age* (Chichester: Polity, 2010).
Markus Schulz, *The Futures We Want: Global Sociology and the Struggles for a Better World* (Berlin: Neopubli, 2016).
Charles Tilly and Lesley Wood, *Social Movements 1768–2012* (London: Routledge, 2012).
Alain Touraine, *The Voice and the Eye: An Analysis of Social Movements* (Cambridge: Cambridge University Press, 1981).

OTHER KINDS OF RESOURCES

Interface: A journal for and about social movements. Open-access activist/academic journal of social movements research; global coverage. http://interfacejournal.org.
COSMOS social movements research centre: resources page at http://cosmos.sns.it/resources/.

Index

police, xi, xiv, 2–3, 5, 12, 16, 19, 21,
  33, 35, 61–62, 82, 84, 87, 103
policy, xiii, 39, 40, 89, 98
political economy, xiii, 36, 90
politics, xiii–xvii, xix, vii, 2–3, 5–6,
  9–13, 17, 19–21, 24–37, 39–41,
  43–49, 52–60, 62–67, 69, 71, 74,
  76–77, 79–80, 84–90, 92, 94–100,
  102–4, 110, 113
poor, 11, 15, 31–32, 45–46, 58, 63,
  68–69, 78, 81, 108
postcolonial, 26, 41, 51, 68, 78, 90
potential, real, 37, 72–75, 99–100, 111
power, xi–xvii, 2–3, 11, 15–27, 29,
  31–37, 40, 47, 50–54, 56, 60, 63,
  66–71, 74, 78–84, 86, 88–92,
  94–97, 99–100, 104–5, 108
practice, xix, vii, 1, 4, 8, 11–12, 38,
  45, 47, 57, 59–62, 64, 71, 73–75,
  86, 91–93, 96, 98, 101–2, 104, 108,
  111–12
praxis, 11, 71, 74–75, 92
privilege, cultural, 3, 15, 75, 81
professionals, xiv, 34, 50, 79, 92, 100
progressive, xix, 30, 33–34, 36, 44, 62,
  67, 95–96
project, xvii, xviii, ix, 1–2, 5, 7–8,
  10–11, 20, 25, 27, 33, 35, 60, 68, 69,
  75, 83, 87, 89, 90, 92–93, 96–97,
  101
psychology, 12, 17, 39, 73, 111

race, 21, 23, 29–30, 44, 56, 64, 66, 81,
  84, 90, 97, 100, 108, 112
racism, xii, 2, 9, 15, 16, 22, 27, 30, 34,
  36, 39, 62, 75, 80–82, 95, 99
radical, xii–xvi, xviii–xix, ix, 6–7,
  16–24, 33–35, 37, 39, 43–47,
  49–50, 52–56, 59–62, 64, 66,
  70–71, 73–75, 79, 81–88, 90–92,
  94, 96, 98–102, 104, 107, 108, 111
radical left, xvii, 7, 18, 50, 58, 62, 85.
  See also left; new left
redistribution, 20–22, 25–27, 29, 49,
  51, 57, 101

refugee, xii, 2, 7, 9, 37, 49, 87
relationship, xiv–xvi, xviii, xix, x, 2,
  10–11, 20, 22, 27, 43–44, 49–50,
  52, 54, 56–57, 59, 62, 64, 66–70,
  73, 79, 85, 89–92, 99, 100, 104–5,
  108–10, 112
religion, xii, 7, 20, 24, 26–27, 29–30,
  32, 36–37, 40, 44–45, 51, 60,
  66–68, 77–82, 84, 86, 108–9
representation, xv, xviii, x, 26, 33, 38,
  49, 56, 86, 97
repression, xii, 42, 47, 49, 55–56,
  70–71
republicanism, Irish, 6, 51, 78–79, 111
research, xvii, xviii, 5, 38–42,
  45–47, 63, 70, 72, 89–94, 96, 98,
  101–4
resistance, xi, xii, xvi, 3, 5–7, 9, 18–19,
  24, 27–29, 31–33, 35–40, 47–48,
  54, 60, 64–65, 67, 70–71, 75–76,
  82, 90, 93, 98–99
resource, xvi, 1, 31, 40, 88
revolution, xi, xii, xvi, xvii, 16–18, 22,
  24, 27, 29, 34–37, 39–40, 47–51,
  54–56, 67, 69, 78–80, 85–86, 88,
  90, 92, 108, 113
right. *See* far right
rights, 7, 9, 12–13, 16, 20–21,
  30–33, 42, 44–45, 49, 78–80, 95,
  103, 109
Rojava. *See* Kurd
routine, xii, xvi, 3–4, 12, 15, 40, 59,
  69–70, 74, 77, 81, 98–101, 108
rural, xii, 7, 35, 58, 68, 84, 103
Russia, 18, 36, 48, 56, 67, 69, 73, 107

Saro-Wiwa, Ken, 31
sexuality, 4, 44, 66, 77, 90, 108, 112
Shell, 31–33, 103
social democracy, xvi, 18, 29, 50, 52
socialism, 9, 18–21, 23, 25–27, 34, 47,
  56, 64–65, 92, 111
social media, 3, 38, 40, 54, 57, 75, 85,
  87, 98
social movement project, 66–70

About the Author

Laurence Cox is one of Europe's leading social movement researchers, senior lecturer in sociology at the National University of Ireland Maynooth and associate researcher at the Collège d'Etudes Mondiales, Paris. He has published widely on different aspects of social movements, including *We Make Our Own History: Marxism and Social Movements in the Twilight of Neoliberalism, Voices of 1968: Documents from the Global North, Understanding European Movements, Marxism and Social Movements* and *Silence Would Be Treason: Last Writings of Ken Saro-Wiwa*. Cox cofounded and coedits the activist/academic social movements journal *Interface*. He has been involved in many different kinds of movement since the 1980s, including ecological, international solidarity, human rights and organising against repression, antiwar, community activism, radical media, self-organised spaces, alternative education and the alter-globalisation 'movement of movements'.